CULTURAL ATLAS FOR YOUNG PEOPLE

FIRST
CIVILIZATIONS

DR. ERICA C. D. HUNTER
UPDATED BY MIKE CORBISHLEY

REVISED EDITION

Facts On File, Inc.

Cultural Atlas for Young People
FIRST CIVILIZATIONS
Revised Edition

Published in North America by:
Facts On File, Inc.
132 West 31st Street
New York NY 10001

AN ANDROMEDA BOOK
Planned and produced by:
Andromeda Oxford Limited
11–13 The Vineyard, Abingdon
Oxfordshire OX14 3PX, United Kingdom
www.andromeda.co.uk

Publishing Director Graham Bateman
Project Manager Kim Richardson
Editor Lionel Bender
Art Director Ben White
Designer Malcolm Smythe
Cartographic Manager Richard Watts
Cartographic Editor Tim Williams
Picture Manager Claire Turner
Picture Researcher Cathy Stastny
Production Director Clive Sparling
Editorial and Administrative Assistants Marian Dreier,
Rita Demetriou
Proofreader Lucy Poddington

Copyright © 2003 Andromeda Oxford Limited

ISBN: 0-8160-5149-6
Set ISBN: 0-8160-5144-5

Facts On File books are available at special discounts
when purchased in bulk quantities for businesses,
associations, institutions or sales promotions. Please
call our Special Sales Department in New York at
(212) 967-8800 or (800) 322-8755.

You can find Facts On File on the World Wide Web at
http://www.factsonfile.com
Originated in Hong Kong
Printed in Hong Kong by Paramount Ltd
10 9 8 7 6 5 4 3 2 1

This book is printed on acid-free paper.

Library of Congress Cataloging-in-Publication Data
available from Facts On File

Artwork and Picture Credits
Maps drafted by Alan Mais, Hornchurch, Essex.

Key: t = top, b = bottom, c = centre, l = left, r = right

Title page M/Erich Lessing. 5 MH. 8 Photo RMN.
8–9 John Hillelson Agency/Georg Gerster. 10 Richard
Hamilton Smith/CORBIS. 12 A&A. 13 Institute of
Archaeology, University of London. 19 Hutchison
Library. 20 SH/F H C Birch. 21 SH. 22t MH. 2
2b MH. 23t MH. 23b MH. 24t Picturepoint.
24bl David Stronach, Berkely. 24br SH. 25 Andromeda.
26 Andromeda. 27tl Andromeda. 27tr Hirmer Verlag.
28l Andromeda. 28r BM. 29 David & Joan Oates.
33 Z/K Goebel. 34t BM. 34–5 Richard and Adam
Hook. 36bl RHPL/V Southwell. 36br Il Quadrante
Edizione, Milan. 36tl Ashmolean Museum. 38d Photo
RMN. 38cr Photo RMN. 38tc John Ridgeway. 38tr John
Ridgeway. 40t Ashmolean Museum. 40b Giraudon.
43t Claus Hansmann. 43cl Charles & Josette Lenars/
CORBIS. 43cr. A&A. 44tc BM. 44tr Scala. 44b AA&A.
45t BM. 45b Scala. 48t Picturepoint. 48b Oriental
Institute Museum, Chicago. 49l Photo RMN.
49r Explorer/Fiore. 50-1 MH. 53t Scala. 53b Claus

Hansmann. 55 Ashmolean Museum. 56 Photo RMN.
57 MH. 59tl MH. 59r MH. 60 Photo RMN.
61 Michael Roaf. 63 Ashmolean Museum. 64 MH.
65tl Photo RMN. 65tr SH. 65dl David Harris.
67 SH/Jane Taylor. 68 Scala. 68–9 Ashmolean Museum.
69 Time Magazine/Barry Iverson. 71r BM. 71b MH.
73 MH. 74 Michael Roaf. 75t Nik Wheeler/CORBIS.
75b MH. 76t Photo RMN. 76b MH. 77 Ashmolean
Museum. 78 Richard and Adam Hook. 79tl Ruggero
Vanni/CORBIS. 79tr BM. 81rl M/Erich Lessing.
81tr Erica C D Hunter. 83t RHPL. 83b RHPL.
85 M/Erich Lessing. 86t MH. 86b M/Erich Lessing.
87 Photo RMN. 88 Michael Roaf. 89 Z. 90t BM.
90b BM. 91tBM. 91bBM.

List of Abbreviations
AA&A Ancient Art & Architecture Collection,
Middlesex, UK. BM British Museum, London, UK.
M Magnum Photos Limited, London, UK.
MH Magnum Photos Limited, London, UK.
MH Michael Holford, Essex, UK. RHPL Robert
Harding Picture Library, London, UK. SH Sonia
Halliday Photographs, Buckinghamshire, UK.
Z Zefa Picture Library, London, UK.

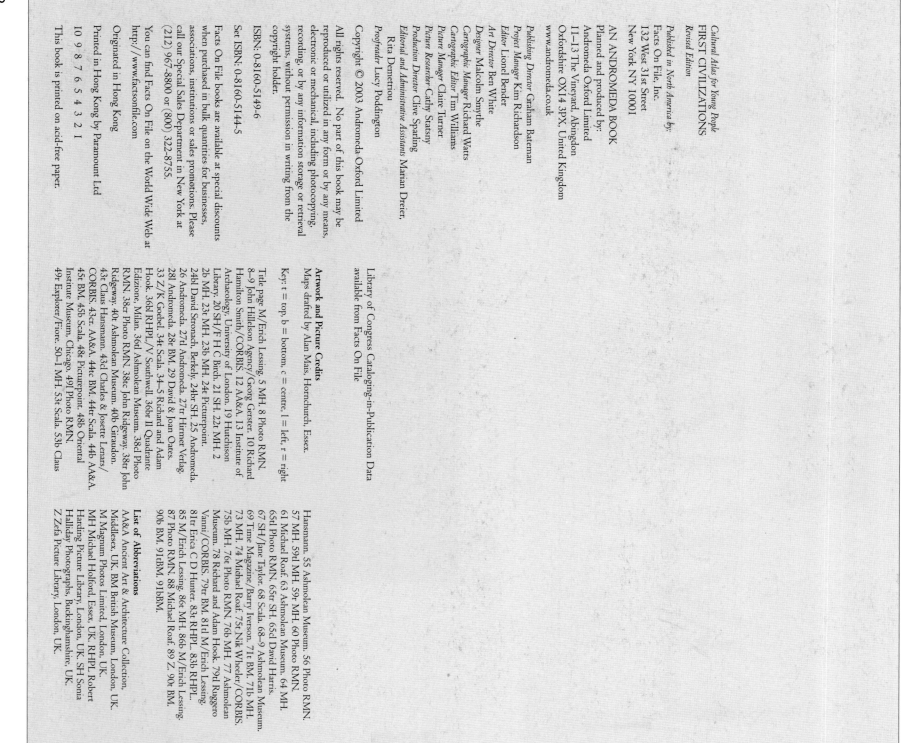

CONTENTS

INTRODUCTION

THIS BOOK IS ABOUT MESOPOTAMIA – THE LAND between the Tigris and Euphrates rivers – and the ancient Near East. It covers the present-day country of Iraq, as well as parts of Iran, Turkey, Syria, Lebanon and Israel. The region is varied in geography and climate, ranging from deserts to forested mountains and fertile river plains.

More than 12,000 years ago people of this region were among the first to change from a hunting-and-gathering, wandering lifestyle to settled farming communities. Many of the plants and animals on which modern European agriculture is based were first domesticated (brought under human control) in the Near East.

The first cities in the world also emerged in Mesopotamia, by about 4000 BCE, and influenced the surrounding cultures. The ancient Greeks and Romans learned from Mesopotamian civilization, and passed on their cultural heritage to Europe. For this reason Mesopotamia has been called the "cradle of civilization."

In recent times the Near East, unique in its contribution to human history, has been the scene of conflict: first the Iran–Iraq War, and then the Gulf War of 1991. Many wars have been fought in Mesopotamia from earliest times. The first kings, dating from about 3000 BCE, were originally leaders chosen by the people to defend city-states in times of war. By 2300 BCE kings had become permanent heads of state, attending not only to military matters but also to the welfare of the population.

Rulers were thought to be responsible to the gods, even though some of them, such as the Assyrian, Babylonian and Persian kings, ruled vast empires. The empire of Darius III was conquered by Alexander the Great in 331 BCE. From then on, the civilization of the ancient Near East went into decline, to be replaced by the newly powerful Hellenistic (Greek-speaking) culture. *First Civilizations* is divided into two parts. Part One,

The Land and the People, traces the development of hunter-gatherer societies through village life to urban (city) life. It describes the domestication of plants and animals, and technological inventions such as clay bricks and pottery and the first writing. Part Two, **Kingdoms and Empires**, charts the rise and fall of the great kingdoms and empires of the Near East. These began with the reign of the Semitic king Sargon of Agade (2334–2279 BCE) and ended with the Persian dynasty.

Most of the evidence for the history of Mesopotamia and the surrounding cultures comes from archeological excavations. Special features in the book focus on the contribution of outstanding sites.

Maps are an important part of the book. In Part One they show where technological changes began and spread in the Near East. In Part Two they show how empires grew and then faded, to be replaced by others. Location maps accompany each special spread, so that the sites may be easily identified.

Many of the pages list the names and dates of the cultures and kings of the period. Kings are usually grouped according to the dynasty (ruling family or line) to which they belonged. The spelling of names is often uncertain, and other versions can be found. Sargon, for example, may also be written as Sharruken. In *First Civilizations* the easiest and most popular form of these names has usually been used. Similarly, many of the dates are not definite and should only be used as an approximate guide.

The Glossary on page 92 explains archeological and technical terms and also defines the names of periods and dynasties. The Gazetteer on page 93 lists sites in alphabetical order, giving their latitude and longitude, as well as their modern locations.

The section entitled Further Reading provides a list of books that we hope will interest you after reading *First Civilizations*.

Abbreviations used in this book
BCE = Before Common Era (also called BC), CE = Common Era (also called AD), c. = circa (about), ch. = chapter, chs = chapters, mi = miles, ft = feet, in = inches.

Right Cuneiform (wedge-shaped) writing carved over the relief sculpture from a 9th-century BCE palace at Kalhu.

TABLE OF DATES

	12,000 BCE	10,000 BCE	7000 BCE	4000 BCE	3000 BCE
ARCHEOLOGICAL PERIOD	EPI-PALEOLITHIC (MESOLITHIC)	PROTO-NEOLITHIC	ACERAMIC NEOLITHIC	NEOLITHIC	SUMERIAN · EARLY BRONZE
ART AND ARCHITECTURE			Round huts; Plastered skulls	Stone sculptures; Rectangular houses; Clay figurines	Tripartite temples; Walled cities; Cone mosaics; "Uruk Mona Lisa"; "Warka vase"; Palaces
MAJOR EVENTS MESOPOTAMIA		End of Ice Age	* Zawi Chemi Shanidar	<u>Hassuna, Samarra, Halaf, Ubaid</u>	<u>Uruk</u>; * Tell Madhhur; * Ur; * Jamdat Nasr; * Mari; <u>Early Dynastic</u>; Nippur; * Uruk
LEVANT	* Mt Carmel		* Jericho	<u>Halaf</u>	<u>Ubaid</u>
IRAN		* Shanidar Cave		* Choga Mami	
ANATOLIA				* Chatal Huyuk	
EGYPT					Pre-Dynastic
TECHNICAL INVENTIONS	Hunting and gathering; Dog domesticated; Microlithic flint tools		Villages; Basketry; Grain roasting; Sheep herded; Farming – grain crops; Mud-bricks; Weaving; Pottery; Early copper tools	Ox-plow; Cattle domesticated; Potter's wheel; Baked mud-bricks; Pottery kilns; Irrigation; Boats	Cities; Donkeys domesticated; Carts; Copper weapons; Cylinder seals; Cuneiform writing; City-states; Lost-wax method of casting metal; Gold- and silversmithing

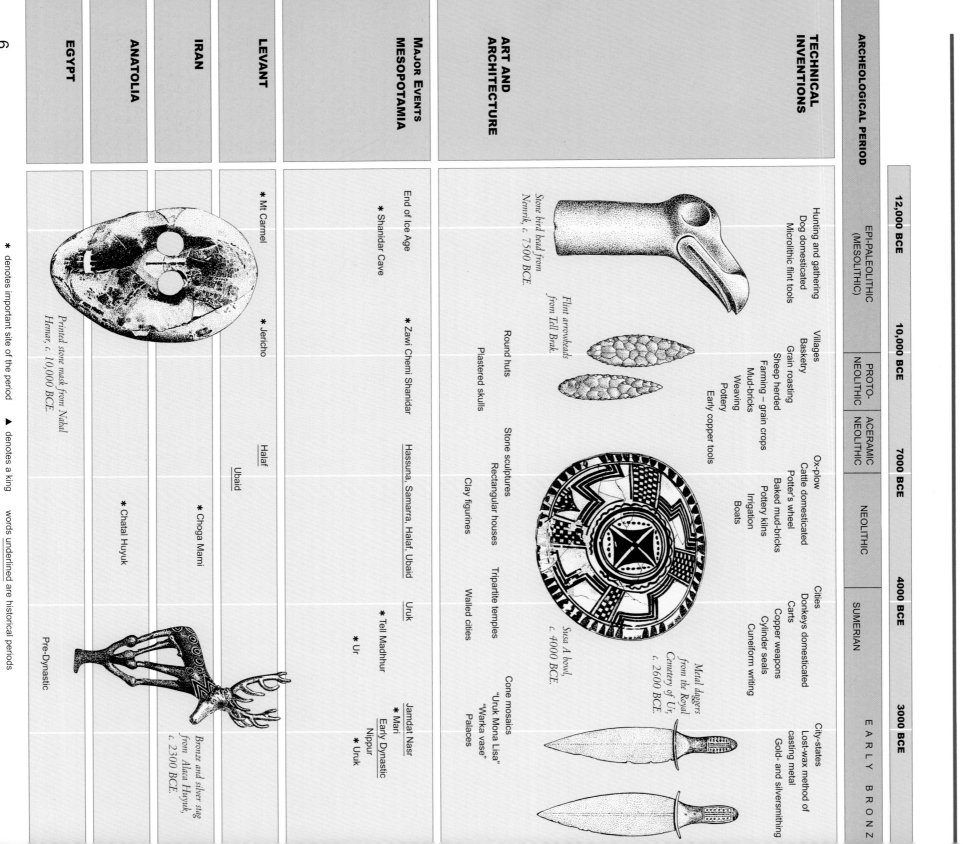

Stone bird head from Nemrik, c. 7500 BCE.

Flint arrowheads from Tell Brak.

Susa A bowl, c. 4000 BCE.

Metal daggers from the Royal Cemetery of Ur, c. 2600 BCE.

Printed stone mask from Nahal Hemar, c. 10,000 BCE.

Bronze and silver stag from Alaca Huyuk, c. 2300 BCE.

* denotes important site of the period   ▲ denotes a king   words underlined are historical periods

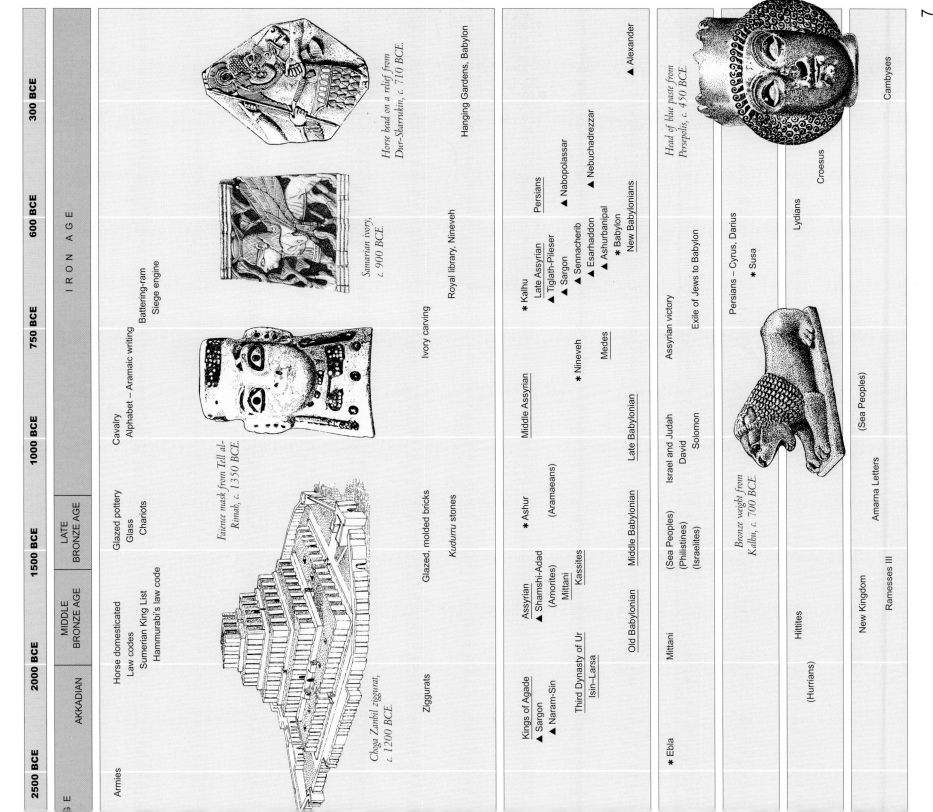

2500 BCE	2000 BCE	1500 BCE	1000 BCE	750 BCE	600 BCE	300 BCE

MIDDLE BRONZE AGE	LATE BRONZE AGE	IRON AGE

G E · AKKADIAN

Armies
Horse domesticated
Law codes
Sumerian King List
Hammurabi's law code

Glazed pottery
Glass
Chariots

Cavalry
Alphabet – Aramaic writing
Battering-ram
Siege engine

Faience mask from Tell al-Rimah, c. 1350 BCE.

Samarian ivory, c. 900 BCE.

Horse head on a relief from Dur-Sharrukin, c. 710 BCE.

Ziggurats
Glazed, molded bricks
Kudurru stones
Ivory carving
Royal library, Nineveh
Hanging Gardens, Babylon

Choga Zanbil ziggurat, c. 1200 BCE.

Kings of Agade
▲ Sargon
▲ Naram-Sin
Third Dynasty of Ur
Isin–Larsa
Old Babylonian

Assyrian
▲ Shamshi-Adad
(Amorites)
Mittani
Kassites
Middle Babylonian

* Ashur
(Aramaeans)
Late Babylonian

Middle Assyrian

* Kalhu
Late Assyrian
▲ Tiglath-Pileser
▲ Sargon
▲ Sennacherib
▲ Esarhaddon
▲ Ashurbanipal
* Babylon
New Babylonians

* Nineveh
Medes

Persians
▲ Nabopolassar
▲ Nebuchadrezzar

▲ Alexander

* Ebla
Mittani

(Sea Peoples)
(Philistines)
(Israelites)
Israel and Judah
David
Solomon

Assyrian victory
Exile of Jews to Babylon

Persians – Cyrus, Darius
* Susa

Bronze weight from Kalhu, c. 700 BCE.

Head of blue paste from Persepolis, c. 450 BCE.

(Hurrians)
Hittites
Amarna Letters
New Kingdom
Ramesses III
(Sea Peoples)

Lydians
Croesus
Cambyses

7

PART ONE

THE LAND AND THE PEOPLE

Above An Akkadian relief from about 2300 BCE showing naked prisoners of war.

Right Stairs leading to the top of the ziggurat at Ur, where once a temple stood.

8

PHYSICAL BACKGROUND

THE LANDS WHERE THE FIRST CIVILIZATIONS developed stretched from The Gulf (often known as the Persian Gulf) through modern Iraq, to Syria and the Levant (present-day Lebanon and Israel) on the Mediterranean coast. This area of the Near East is often called the Fertile Crescent.

The heartland of this cradle of human history was Mesopotamia – the flat plain of rich soil that was watered by the Tigris and Euphrates rivers. These two rivers rise in the mountainous region of northeastern Turkey and drain into The Gulf.

The Zagros Mountains in modern Iran formed the eastern barrier to this region. In the west and south were the desolate lands of the Syrian and Arabian deserts.

CLIMATE AND ENVIRONMENT

When the last Ice Age ended, in about 12,000 BCE, the climate of the Near East became similar to what it is today. The vegetation (plant life) changed because of the warmer temperatures.

The mountains of Iran, Turkey, and the Mediterranean coast became forested with oak, cedar, and pine trees. These woods and forests became the home of deer, wild sheep and goats, wolves, and leopards. Wild wheat and barley also grew here.

The northern part of Mesopotamia consisted of rolling grasslands where boars, oxen, and even lions roamed. The southern part of Mesopotamia, towards The Gulf, hosted a wealth of bird life that lived in its many swamps and marshes.

WATER

People could only live permanently in the areas where there were constant supplies of water. Rainfall was scarce in Mesopotamia, but the Tigris and Euphrates were mighty rivers, fed by the melting snows of the Zagros and Taurus mountains. With their many lesser, tributary rivers, they provided a lifeline throughout Mesopotamia. Irrigation canals were cut from the rivers and their tributaries to bring the water directly to the fields.

Left An oasis in the desert. Oases – areas that are fertile because water is present – are quite common in deserts. Often the water comes from an underground spring. Palm trees occur naturally at oases, and with irrigation crops can be grown, allowing orchards and gardens to thrive.

IRRIGATION

Unlike the river Nile, which flooded Egypt with such regularity that it could be calculated, the Tigris and Euphrates were unpredictable and unreliable. They could rise in flood, becoming raging muddy torrents, or change their courses overnight and in doing so destroy the villages that lined their banks.

In time, the people of the river plains learned to build irrigation systems (canals and ditches) that helped them control the flow of water and channel it to their food crops. Then the "land between the rivers" (which is what the Greek name Mesopotamia means) became highly productive for farming.

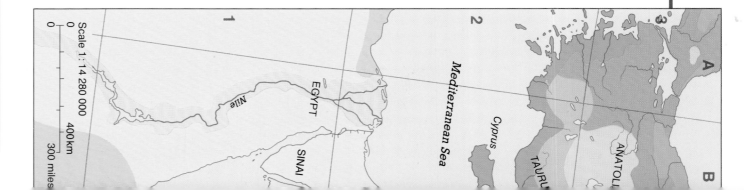

Scale 1 : 14 280 000

0
0

400km

300 miles

1

2

A
3

B

Mediterranean Sea

Cyprus

ANATOL

TAURU

EGYPT

SINAI

Nile

Above Land and vegetation of the Near East. This map shows the natural vegetation, that is, how the vegetation would be if left alone, without human interference. The vegetation depends mainly on the pattern of rainfall. Large areas of the Near East receive so little rain that the land is desert and not suitable for human settlement. Fringes of the desert are steppe grasslands.

Left Annual rainfall in the Near East. The region is mainly dry and hot. It receives no rain during the summer months from June to September. Temperatures are high and in the lower-lying zones often reach 113°F. In winter, snow falls on the mountains of the Levant, Turkey, and Iran.

Natural vegetation

- Coniferous forest
- Deciduous forest
- Mixed forest
- Mediterranean forest
- Floodplain
- Steppe
- Semi-desert
- Desert

Mean annual rainfall (inches)

- 40
- 24
- 16
- 8
- 4
- 0

Scale 1 : 31 500 000

0   800km
0   500 miles

Black Sea

CAUCASUS MTS

Caspian Sea

Kara Kum

Amu Darya

ELBURZ MTS

Dasht-e Kavir

Dasht-e Lut

ZAGROS MOUNTAINS

ELAM

The Gulf

Gulf of Oman

Kizil Irmak

SYRIA

Great Zab

Tigris

Habur

Euphrates

MESOPOTAMIA

SYRIAN DESERT

An Nafud

ARABIA

HEJAZ

Red Sea

Black Sea

Mediterranean Sea

Caspian Sea

Euphrates

Tigris

The Gulf

Red Sea

11

ARCHEOLOGY IN THE NEAR EAST

ARCHEOLOGY IS THE SCIENTIFIC STUDY OF the human past using the physical traces left by early people. This has told us a lot about the history of the Near East. In the 19th century, archeologists from Europe and America dug up sites to find objects for their museums. Today, archeology tries to reconstruct from its findings how society was organized.

EXCAVATING A SITE

Archeologists do a variety of jobs, from supervising the people who physically dig the site to recording every detail about the different levels that are exposed. The oldest remains are usually at the lowest levels, with the most recent closest to the surface.

Archeological "finds" may range from gold coins and beautiful jewelry to hundreds or thousands of pieces of broken pottery, fragments of animal bones, and tools made of stone (flint). Even the seeds of plants are collected, by passing the soil in which they are found through sieves. Seeds give information about crops and foods. Important finds that are broken are repaired, and there are special treatments for ivory, wood, metal items, and inscriptions (carved or engraved words).

The contours (outline) of excavated sites used to be mapped by hand, but nowadays they are often charted using a computer. More and more advanced scientific techniques are being used in archeology today, including new discoveries by satellite photography (using infrared film).

12

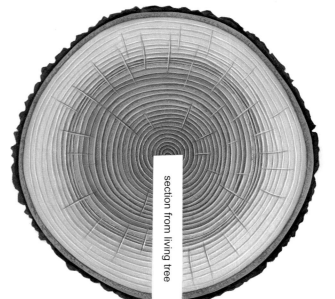

Below The trunk of a tree shows a number of rings when it is sawn in half. Each ring equals a year's growth: the warmer the conditions in any year, the wider the ring will be.

By adding up the number of rings, the age of the tree can be worked out, even if it is hundreds or thousands of years old. Sequences of tree rings where the years of growth are known can be matched with the ring patterns of an ancient piece of timber, telling us how old it is.

section from living tree

time back in past

rings match

sequences from older timber

rings match

sequence from living tree

Right A worker uses a paintbrush to dust away the soil from pieces of pottery. The woman is placing these pieces, called sherds, into the rubber basket. The pottery is taken away and washed carefully so that any decoration or inscriptions will not be removed. The location of each sherd is noted to help work out their relationship.

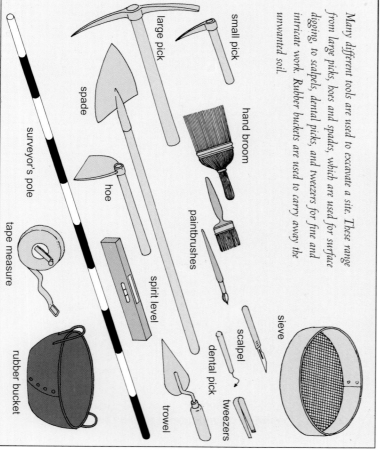

Many different tools are used to excavate a site. These range from large picks, hoes and spades, which are used for surface digging, to scalpels, dental picks, and tweezers for fine and intricate work. Rubber buckets are used to carry away the unwanted soil.

large pick

small pick

spade

hand broom

hoe

paintbrushes

spirit level

sieve

scalpel

dental pick

tweezers

trowel

surveyor's pole

tape measure

rubber bucket

BUILDING UP A PICTURE FROM THE SITE

The layout of the buildings in the different layers of the excavation shows archeologists how the site developed. Major features, such as city walls and gates, may show similarities with other sites and help to establish the site's dating sequence or chronology.

The chronology also can be worked out from the pottery that was found, because certain shapes were used in different periods. Coins are very useful for working out the date of a site, but coins are not found in periods earlier than the 7th century BCE. Inscriptions may also supply historical information.

Radio carbon dating, a sophisticated scientific technique, can show the age of wooden objects. However, the results may not be of great value for dating a site, because the objects may originally have come from elsewhere. They may therefore show trade links between the excavated site and other areas of the Near East. Pottery excavated from the site may supply similar evidence. Pottery can be dated by thermoluminescence which measures the decay of radioactive elements in the clay.

Left Archeologists at work. The team have unearthed the stone wall topped by the layers of mud-brick. After they have drawn it, they will demolish it to find out what is underneath. A worker climbs the ladder with a bucket of soil, which is dumped on to the nearby piles. The dagger, skeleton, broken pots, and other items will be uncovered as the lower levels are excavated.

Below Fragile objects that are found have to be very carefully treated. These statuettes were made from mud plastered on a reed framework. The intricate process of sticking together all the fragments is a painstaking and expensive job that takes months.

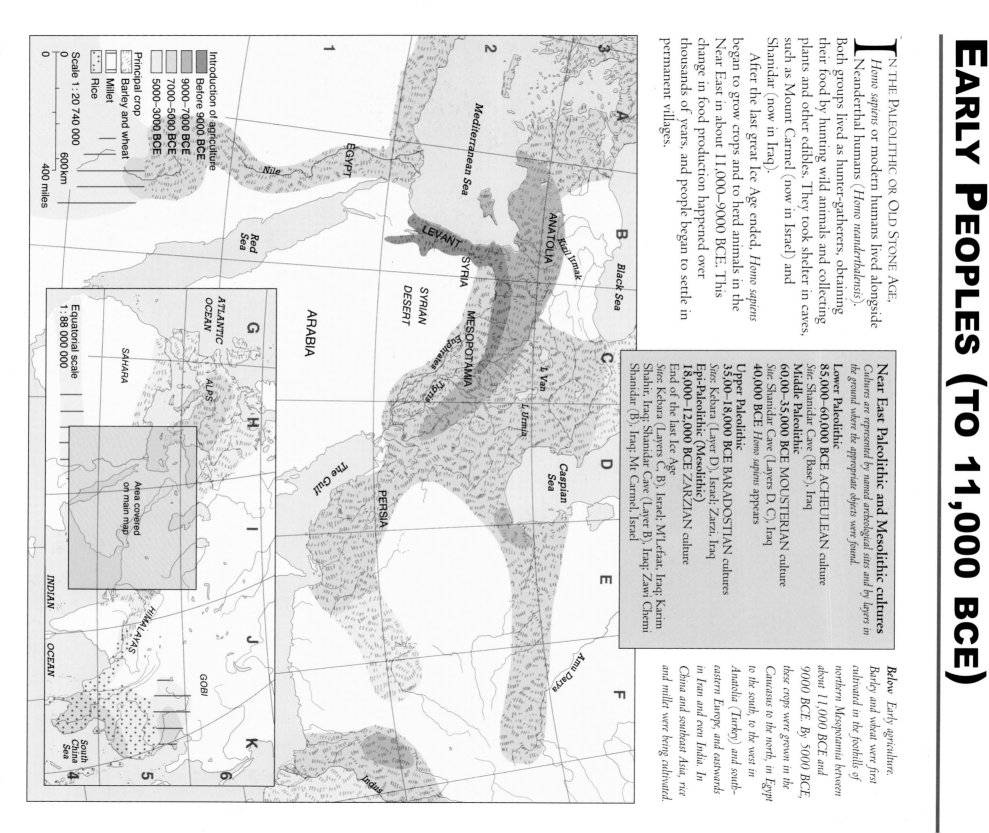

IN THE PALEOLITHIC OR OLD STONE AGE, *Homo sapiens* or modern humans lived alongside Neanderthal humans (*Homo neanderthalensis*). Both groups lived as hunter-gatherers, obtaining their food by hunting wild animals and collecting plants and other edibles. They took shelter in caves, such as Mount Carmel (now in Israel) and Shanidar (now in Iraq).

After the last great Ice Age ended, *Homo sapiens* began to grow crops and to herd animals in the Near East in about 11,000–9000 BCE. This change in food production happened over thousands of years, and people began to settle in permanent villages.

Near East Paleolithic and Mesolithic cultures

Cultures are represented by named archeological sites and by layers in the ground where the appropriate objects were found.

Lower Paleolithic
85,000–60,000 BCE ACHEULEAN culture
Site: Shanidar Cave (Base), Iraq
Middle Paleolithic
60,000–35,000 BCE MOUSTERIAN culture
Site: Shanidar Cave (Layers D, C), Iraq
40,000 BCE *Homo sapiens* appears
Upper Paleolithic
35,000–18,000 BCE BARADOSTIAN cultures
Sites: Kebara (Layer D), Israel; Zarzi, Iraq
Epi-Paleolithic (Mesolithic)
18,000–12,000 BCE ZARZIAN culture
End of the last Ice Age
Sites: Kebara (Layers C, B), Israel; M'Lefaat, Iraq; Karim Shahir, Iraq; Shanidar Cave (Layer B), Iraq; Zawi Chemi Shanidar (B), Iraq; Mt Carmel, Israel

Below Early agriculture. Barley and wheat were first cultivated in the foothills of northern Mesopotamia between about 11,000 BCE and 9000 BCE. By 5000 BCE, these crops were grown in the Caucasus to the north, in Egypt to the south, to the west in Anatolia (Turkey) and southeastern Europe, and eastwards in Iran and even India. In China and southeast Asia, rice and millet were being cultivated.

Introduction of agriculture
Before 9000 BCE
9000–7000 BCE
7000–5000 BCE
5000–3000 BCE

Principal crop
Barley and wheat
Millet
Rice

Scale 1:20 740 000
0
0
600 km
400 miles

Equatorial scale
1:88 000 000

Area covered on main map

14

Mediterranean Sea · Nile · EGYPT · Red Sea · ARABIA · LEVANT · SYRIA · ANATOLIA · Kizil Irmak · Black Sea · SYRIAN DESERT · MESOPOTAMIA · Euphrates · Tigris · L Van · L Urmia · Caspian Sea · PERSIA · The Gulf · Amu Darya · HIMALAYAS · ALPS · SAHARA · ATLANTIC OCEAN · INDIAN OCEAN · GOBI · South China Sea · Indus

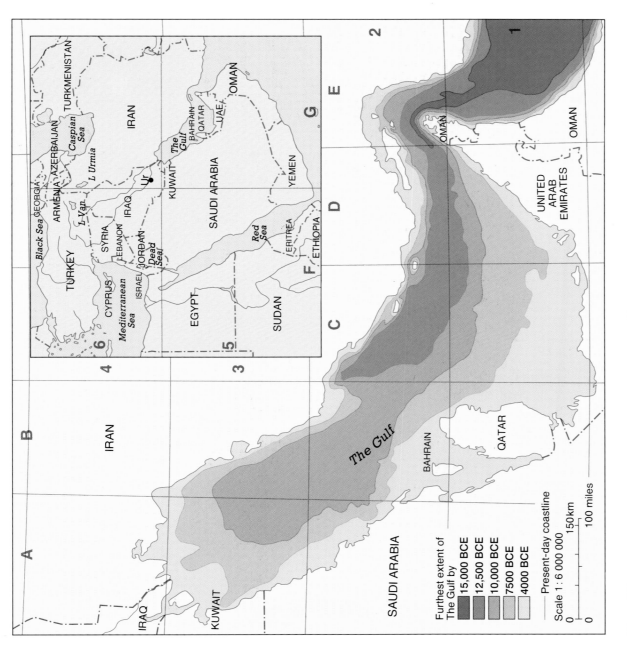

Right The changing shape of The Gulf. The Gulf has been growing in size since 15,000 BCE, when sea levels were about 330ft lower than today. As the last Ice Age ended, sea levels rose with the warmer temperatures. Since 4000 BCE sea levels have remained almost the same, but silting from the Tigris and Euphrates rivers has changed the coastline. These maps show the boundaries of present-day countries.

Furthest extent of The Gulf by
- 15,000 BCE
- 12,500 BCE
- 10,000 BCE
- 7500 BCE
- 4000 BCE

— Present-day coastline

Scale 1 : 6 000 000

0 — 150km

0 — 100 miles

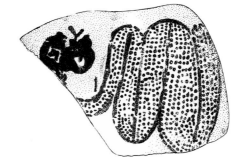

Above A snake painted on a piece of pottery dating from before 5000 BCE. Many such pottery decorations show the wild animals and birds that lived in the ancient Near East.

THE NEOLITHIC REVOLUTION

The change from hunter-gatherer societies transformed the human lifestyle and is known as the "Neolithic revolution" (Neolithic means New Stone Age). The first settlements were in Palestine and the upper Euphrates valley of Syria. They seem to have developed separately rather than coming from a single center.

Climatic changes that took place in the Near East after the last Ice Age resulted in higher temperatures, different forms of vegetation and, perhaps, fewer animals. In the warmer temperatures the human population increased. The combination of these events may have helped trigger the Neolithic revolution.

STONE TECHNOLOGY

To cater for the new methods of food production new tools had to be developed. Most tools were made from flint or other stone using such techniques as chipping, flaking, "pecking," and grinding.

Towards the end of the Paleolithic period, very small flints appeared. Called microliths, these come in different shapes. Some set in bone sickle handles (curved cutting tools) have been found at Mount Carmel. Microlith flints were sharper and more efficient than the larger tools of the Paleolithic or Old Stone Age. They show that people collected grains, but do not prove that they already cultivated plants.

SHANIDAR

S HANIDAR CAVE IS LOCATED NEAR THE Great Zab river in the rugged Zagros Mountains of Iraqi Kurdistan. As early as 100,000 BCE small groups of Neanderthal people sheltered here during the cold winter months. They hunted wild sheep, pigs, cattle, and goats.

Several of the cave-dwellers were killed by rockfalls. Pollen deposits found with skeletons show that Neanderthal people may have also buried their dead, sometimes with flowers. Their stone tools belong to the Middle Paleolithic Mousterian culture.

Modern humans (*Homo sapiens*) appeared at Shanidar in about 40,000 BCE. Their tools were much more advanced than those of the Neanderthals, who died out by 33,000 BCE. There are no signs of people living at Shanidar between 28,000 BCE and 12,000 BCE. Later tools from the Epi-Paleolithic culture found there are made of obsidian (a dark, glassy, volcanic rock), indicating trade with southeast Turkey. Twenty-six skeletons, some with grave goods, were buried in the cave in about 10,000 BCE. One of the skeletons, that of a man, had had his arm amputated, perhaps because of a disease or injury.

Below *Life at Zawi Chemi Shanidar. Hunters are gathered around the fire. One is making a flint spearhead, by flaking it into a sharp point. Another man has been collecting firewood from the nearby oak forests. The men wear garments made from animal skins. Skins were also used for the roofs of the round huts.*

Shanidar

ZAWI CHEMI SHANIDAR

Zawi Chemi Shanidar, 1.8mi from Shanidar Cave, bridges the period between the Epi-Paleolithic and the first fully developed villages, such as Jarmo. The stone tools used were similar to earlier ones, but new types also emerged. As at Shanidar Cave, there was some trading in types of stone used for toolmaking.

At three different periods, round huts of about 13ft in diameter were built of river boulders. People may have lived at Zawi Chemi Shanidar through the summer and returned to Shanidar Cave for the

winter. Pollen samples suggest that wild wheat and barley were being cultivated. We know that sheep were being herded from about 10,000 BCE because the bones of a number of young animals have been found. The discovery of remains of older animals would have suggested that the people of Zawi Chemi Shanidar were hunting, not herding, sheep.

A pile of eagles' wingbones and 15 goats' skulls were found at the site. This suggests that people practiced religious ceremonies there. Zawi Chemi Shanidar was settled at the same time as many sites in the Levant but there are no direct links.

Below Women at Zawi Chemi Shanidar scrape and stretch the skin of a red deer. They may have also made the fiber baskets, used for collecting such food as snails, outside the hut doorways. Goats or sheep are kept behind the wicker fence.

B Y 10,000 BCE PEOPLE BEGAN TO SETTLE IN villages. Many of these villages were very small, covering less than 2.5 acres (about the area of a small field). Round huts were built sunk partly into the ground for insulation against extremes of heat and cold. The earliest group of round huts dates from as long ago as 15,000 BCE at Ain Gev, on the banks of the Sea of Galilee. Much later, houses became rectangular with plastered walls, and they sometimes had several rooms. Both stages of housing were found among the 26 levels of occupation at Beidha in present-day southern Jordan.

TOOLS, MATERIALS, AND CRAFTS

People still made many tools from stone. Some had chisel edges and may have been used to cut wood, which was then fashioned into other tools. Wooden implements may have been used in harvesting or for animal traps. Unlike stone, wood decays, but at Nahal Hemar in modern Israel a wooden-handled sickle has been found.

Bone and horn from slaughtered animals made a variety of tools that were used for fishing, the preparation of hides (animal skins) and basketry, weaving, and rope-making. Evidence of matting dating from as early as 10,000 BCE has been found

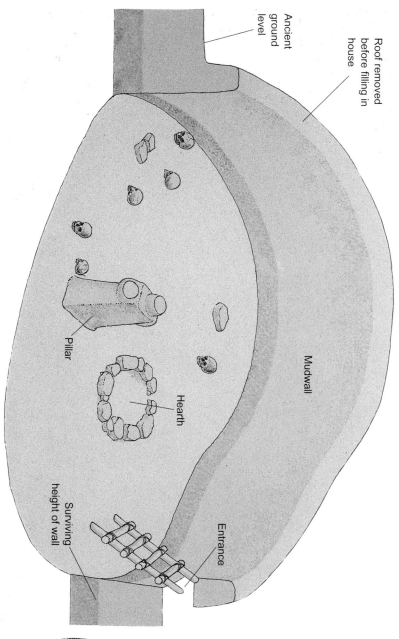

Ancient ground level

Roof removed before filling in house

Pillar

Mudwall

Hearth

Surviving height of wall

Entrance

Below This round house at Qermez Dere in northern Iraq was built partly sunk into the ground. Sunken houses were easier to build and also had better insulation against the climate. The roof, possibly made of skins, may have been held up by wooden poles. The stone walls were covered with mud. Cooking was done on the hearth. The stone-and-plaster pillar and the skulls indicate that ritual cults had developed.

NAHAL HEMAR

Some very useful finds have been made at Nahal Hemar, a cave in the Judaean desert near the Dead Sea. Until this discovery was made in 1938, the only evidence of reed matting and basketry was a few impressions left in clay.

Although archeologists found that the people did not use or make clay pots, they did discover in the cave fragments of textiles, wood, and basketry dating from about 7000 BCE. They had been preserved by the dry climate. Hundreds of pieces of cord, ranging from fine string to thick rope, show the high technical skills of the people at this site. Baskets made from coils of twisted cord and coated in bitumen (a naturally occurring tar) may have been used to carry and store water.

Among the ritual or religious objects unearthed at Nahal Hemar were a stone mask with a human head, heads made of wood and clay, four small carved bone human heads, and several adult skulls. These items may have been part of a cult of ancestor-worship, which was common among early peoples.

at Shanidar Cave. Tools used by North American Indian tribes today show how these crafts were practiced.

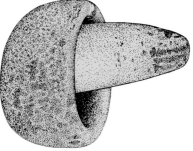

Below Stone mortars and pestles have been found at many sites throughout the Near East. They were used to grind grain and to prepare pigments such as brownish yellow ochre for decoration. Similar-shaped implements are used in modern kitchens today.

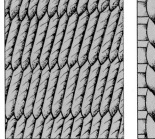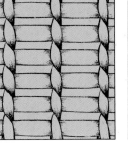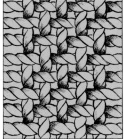

made of matting laid upon timber beams, can be used for living space, sleeping, and storage.

Left Modern houses in villages in the Near East are still built of mud-brick today. Their flat roofs, which are

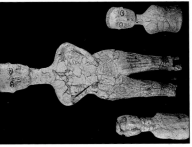

Left Male and female statuettes from a large collection found at Ain Ghazal, near Amman in Jordan. They are made of reed plastered with clay. The exact purpose of these figures is unknown, but must have been linked to rituals or religious practice.

WIDESPREAD RITUAL CULTS

Plastered and decorated skulls, sometimes with shells in their eye sockets, have been found at many sites from the same period in the Levant, including Jericho, Am Mallaha, Mount Carmel, and Ain Chazal. The skulls were buried under the floors of houses. At Nemrik, in northern Mesopotamia, 15 stylized stone sculptures of birds, animals, and humans were discovered. These may have been totems (symbolic objects used in rituals).

Right Textiles were woven from plant fibers, probably flax (linen), in several ways. Pairs of weft threads were twisted around the warps to produce a dense weave called close twining (top). With spaced twining, the twisted threads were separated (center). Normal or tabby weaving (below) was also carried out. Weaving was done by hand, using tools made from the long bones of animals. Shuttles that were pointed at one end and pierced with a hole at the other have been found at Ghassul in Jordan.

Below Points for spears or harpoons, arrowheads, pins, needles, awls, and hooks were made from bone, stone, and wood. It is not certain why grooves were carved into some of them.

Below Sickles were used to cut grasses and reeds. They were often made from bone. The tiny microlith flint blades were fixed to the handle with bitumen.

FIRST FARMERS (11,000–9300 BCE)

THE NEAR EAST WAS ONE OF THE FIRST regions in the world where agriculture developed. Wild ancestors of the grains that were cultivated and the animals that were domesticated first appeared in the Levant and on the hills flanking the north Mesopotamian and Syrian plains.

GRAIN COLLECTION

The Neolithic revolution in the Levant began about 11,000 BCE with the Natufian period. Sickles and grinding stones from this period found at Mount Carmel, on the shores of the Mediterranean, indicate that cereals were an important part of the diet. At Ain Mallaha, in Syria, a number of bell-shaped storage pits were discovered. These were lined with plaster and used to store grain. At Mureybet in northern Syria there were pits to roast grain. It is not known whether these cereals were cultivated or only gathered.

Left The first farmers probably winnowed their grain (to separate edible grain from outer chaff) as this present-day Arab farmer. His fork may be based on an ancient design. Few early wooden tools have been found.

Below Settlements and farmers. After the last Ice Age, people began to establish villages in areas of good rainfall (more than 8in a year) where cereals grew naturally and animals were plentiful. Such early village sites span the Fertile Crescent from the Levant through northern Syria to Iraqi Kurdistan.

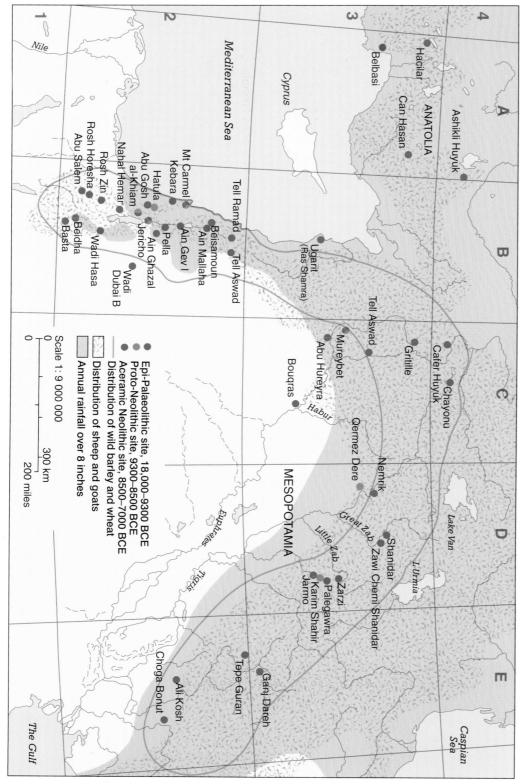

Nile

Mediterranean Sea

Cyprus

ANATOLIA

MESOPOTAMIA

Caspian Sea

The Gulf

Lake Van

L Urmia

Great Zab

Little Zab

Habur

Euphrates

Tigris

Sites
Belbasi
Haclar
Can Hasan
Ashikli Huyuk
Mt Carmel
Kebara
Hatula
Abu Gosh
al-Khiam
Nahal Hemar
Rosh Zin
Rosh Horesha
Abu Salem
Beidha
Basta
Wadi Hasa
Wadi Dubai B
Jericho
Ain Ghazal
Pella
Ain Gev I
Ain Mallaha
Beisamoun
Tell Ramad
Tell Aswad
Ugarit (Ras Shamra)
Mureybet
Abu Hureyra
Tell Aswad
Grtille
Cafer Huyuk
Chayonu
Qermez Dere
Nemrik
Bouqras
Shanidar
Zawi Chemi Shanidar
Zarzi
Palegawra
Karim Shahir
Jarmo
Ganj Dareh
Tepe Guran
Ali Kosh
Choga Bonut

Legend
- Epi-Palaeolithic site, 18,000–9300 BCE
- Proto-Neolithic site, 9300–8500 BCE
- Aceramic Neolithic site, 8500–7000 BCE
- Distribution of wild barley and wheat
- Distribution of sheep and goats
- Annual rainfall over 8 inches

Scale 1 : 9 000 000

0   300 km
0   200 miles

Right The Taurus Mountains dominate this valley in Cilicia, southern Turkey. It lies in the rainfall zone where crops could be grown in the fields without irrigation. Herds could graze in the pastures during the winter months and in the summer were taken up the mountains to feed. The environment provides a year-round food supply.

Below Stages in the domestication of wheat in the Near East. Emmer wheat was a natural hybrid (cross-bred offspring) of einkorn wheat and goat grass. Further selective breeding helped produce wheat plants ideal for harvesting and threshing.

Grain-gathering cultures of the Levant during the Epi-Paleolithic (Mesolithic) period, 18,000–9300 BCE

Cultures are represented by named archeological sites.

18,000–11,000 BCE KEBARAN culture
Site: Kebara, Israel

15,000 BCE First evidence of round huts and mortars
Site: Ain Gev, Israel

12,000 BCE End of last Ice Age (Pleistocene)

11,000 BCE Seasonal or permanent settlement in northern Mesopotamia
Site: Zawi Chemi Shanidar, Iraq

11,000–9300 BCE NATUFIAN culture
Seasonal or permanent settlement, with milling and roasting of grain
Sites: Mt Carmel, Israel; Ain Mallaha, Syria; Beidha, Jordan; Abu Hureyra, Syria

GRAIN CULTIVATION

The Natufian diet included wild barley and two kinds of wheat that grew naturally in the Near East. Einkorn wheat and emmer wheat must have provided the seed for the first crops. Domestic varieties of wheat were developed over generations of selective planting and harvesting. Other cereals, such as barley, were also bred to create strains that yielded more seed. This selection process helped people to produce more food. By 8000 BCE most communities in the Near East grew cereals.

ANIMAL HUSBANDRY

In various parts of the world the earliest peoples gradually developed herding, then farming techniques. They hunted to supplement their diet. We cannot tell exactly when people first bred animals – the process of domestication took several thousand years and was complicated. Many animals that were native to the Near East were eventually domesticated: for example, wolves were domesticated to become dogs, "mouflons" became sheep, and aurochs (wild cattle) became cows. Natufian sites including Mount Carmel and Abu Hureyra in Syria show that wild animals (gazelle, boar, deer) were commonly eaten. Large numbers of bones from young animals suggest that herding and selective culling (choosing which animals would remain in the herd) may have taken place.

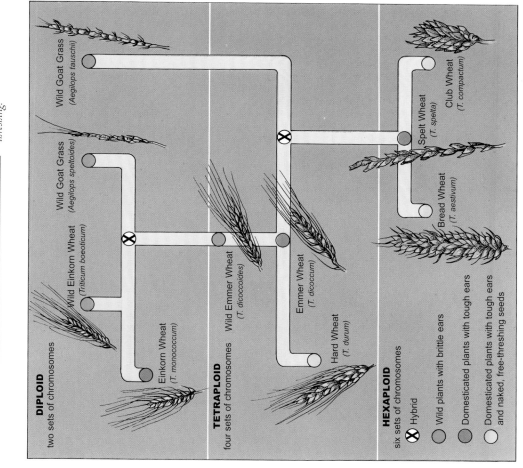

DIPLOID two sets of chromosomes
Wild Einkorn Wheat (*Triticum boeoticum*)
Einkorn Wheat (*T. monococcum*)
Wild Goat Grass (*Aegilops speltoides*)
Wild Goat Grass (*Aegilops tauschii*)

TETRAPLOID four sets of chromosomes
Wild Emmer Wheat (*T. dicoccoides*)
Emmer Wheat (*T. dicoccum*)
Hard Wheat (*T. durum*)

HEXAPLOID six sets of chromosomes
Spelt Wheat (*T. spelta*)
Club Wheat (*T. compactum*)
Bread Wheat (*T. aestivum*)

⊗ Hybrid
○ Wild plants with brittle ears
● Domesticated plants with tough ears
○ Domesticated plants with tough ears and naked, free-threshing seeds

DOGS SEEM TO HAVE BEEN THE FIRST animals that were tamed. A dog's jawbone from 11,000 BCE has been found at Palegawra in northeastern Iraq. At Ain Mallaha a skeleton of a young puppy dated to 10,000 BCE was buried in a grave with a woman. Dogs were domesticated from wolves and probably helped people hunt wild animals.

SHEEP AND GOATS

Not all wild animals could be domesticated. Large amounts of bones left at Natufian sites in the Levant show that gazelles were a major part of the diet. At Abu Hureyra villagers were hunting gazelles and harvesting wild cereals around 9500 BCE. Attempts to herd gazelles seem to have failed, and instead sheep, which were not native to the region, were introduced from northern zones.

Sheep and goats formed an important part of the farming economy, providing meat, hides, milk, and fleece. The first domestic sheep appear in about 11,000 BCE at Zawi Cheni Shanidar. Goats were domesticated at Tepe Asiab, in the Zagros Mountains.

These animals also had a ritual or religious importance. Goats' skulls were found at Zawi Cheni Shanidar, along with wing bones of large birds. Two rams' skulls were found attached, one above the other, to the walls of a shrine at Ganj Dareh.

Origin of common farm animals

Domesticated animal	Wild ancestor	Region	Date
Dog	Wolf	Near East	c. 11,000 BCE
Goat	Bezoar goat	Near East	c. 8500 BCE
Sheep	Asiatic mouflon	Near East	c. 8000 BCE
Pig	Wild boar	Near East	c. 7500 BCE
Cattle	Auroch	Near East	c. 7000 BCE
Cat	Wild cat	Near East	c. 7000 BCE
Chicken	Red jungle fowl	China	c. 6000 BCE
Llama	Guanaco	Andes	c. 5000 BCE
Donkey	Wild ass	Near East	c. 4000 BCE
Horse	Tarpan	Southern Russia	c. 4000 BCE
Camel	Wild camel	?Southern Arabia/Southern Central Asia	c. 3000 BCE
Guinea-pig	Cavy	Peru	c. 2000 BCE
Rabbit	Wild rabbit	Spain	c. 1000 BCE
Turkey	Wild turkey	Mexico	c. 300 BCE

Above A procession of goats, sheep, and cattle, inlaid in bone on the "Standard of Ur" (probably the sounding box of a musical instrument). The men's clothes shown here were made from the fine wool of domesticated sheep, which was much softer than the rough hairy fleece of wild sheep.

Below Arab warriors on camels fleeing from the Assyrian army. Camels were introduced into Mesopotamia from Arabia between 2000 BCE and 1000 BCE. They were used for transport and war.

CATTLE

Wild cattle (aurochs) roamed the Near East and were hunted for their meat and hides. At Chatal Hüyuk in central Turkey, cattle were domesticated by 6000 BCE. They were an important source of food and make up 90 percent of the animal bones found at this site.

Bulls' skulls have been found in several shrines. In one, they were near a painting of vultures attacking headless corpses. At Mureybit in northern Syria, fragments of an ox's skull were deliberately buried in a clay bench. In Anatolia the bull became associated with the weather or storm god.

Right A fine relief of a mastiff being taken out hunting. Hunting dogs were bred for size and strength. Dog skeletons found in graves at Eridu, Iraq, and dating from about 5000 BCE have been identified as greyhounds. They are the ancestors of the saluki, which is still prized today in Arabia for its hunting skills.

Left A 9th-century BCE carving showing horses being groomed and fed. The onager or wild ass was native to the Near East. But the horse only arrived from the central Russian steppes in about 4000 BCE. Horses were used at first to pull chariots. In Sumerian times (about 2500 BCE) they were thought to be inferior beasts which no gentleman would ride. A king or a noble would ride in a chariot pulled by asses. By 1000 BCE, however, cavalry formed very effective fighting units.

BUILDERS AND TRADE

PEOPLE FIRST USED UNBAKED MUD-BRICK FOR building in about 8000 BCE. It was cheap, easy to make, and more readily available than stone. The earliest bricks, from the Proto-Neolithic period (the earliest Neolithic), were made by hand and looked like a loaf of bread, with a flat base and a rounded top. Much later, houses became rectangular in shape when straight-sided mud-bricks were used.

JERICHO

People lived at Jericho, in the Jordan valley, from 9000 BCE. Round huts built from cigar-shaped handmade bricks provide the earliest known use of mud-bricks. In about 8000 BCE a huge, thick, stone wall was erected, surrounded by a large ditch. There was also a massive tower with a staircase inside. The wall and tower were probably built for defense and were recalled in the later biblical story of Joshua.

Above Later, mud-bricks became straight-sided, made from a mixture of mud, chopped straw, and water. The mixture is placed in a mold, then left to dry in the sun for several days.

Right Mud-bricks are still used in the Near East. Their shape and size have varied from period to period, so bricks can help to date a building. Square bricks were easier to use than other shapes.

Right An early mud-brick, shaped by the brick-maker's hand. He has pressed his thumbs into the top, leaving a herring-bone pattern. This was not decoration, but done to fix the mortar and to let it "breathe."

Right The city of Erbil in Iraqi Kurdistan stands on a mound over 165ft high. Mud-brick buildings decay and collapse in the climate of the Near East. New houses are built on the remains of the old ones. After many centuries the debris forms a mound, called a tell. On the flat Mesopotamian landscape, tells are very noticeable.

USING METALS AND CLAY

Major changes happened in about 8500 BCE. At Chayonu in Anatolia (modern Turkey), more than 100 copper beads, pins, and tools have been found. Copper may have come from a local source of ore rather than being smelted. Copper beads have also been discovered in the Zagros Mountains, at Ali Kosh.

At the nearby site of Ganj Dareh, the rectangular buildings were made of long, handmade mud-bricks. Many human and animal figurines (small figures) modeled in clay and pottery vessels have also been found there.

At Mureybet, at the western end of the Fertile Crescent, four lightly fired pots were found in a house. This pottery can be dated to 8000 BCE and

Above Skulls were sometimes inlaid in the eye sockets of skulls buried under the floors of houses at Jericho. The skull was separated from the skeleton after the rest of the body had decayed.

is 500 years older than any other examples. A new industry had begun in the Near East. It signaled a major step in the history of technical development.

TRADE

Jericho, an oasis town of about 1,500 people, grew rich through farming crops and hunting animals. However, it may also have been a trading center for salt and bitumen from the nearby Dead Sea, cowrie shells from the Red Sea, and turquoise and copper from the Sinai peninsula. All these products were widely traded throughout the Near East. Obsidian was found at Jericho and at other sites as far away as Jarmo in Iraqi Kurdistan. This volcanic glass, with a much sharper cutting edge than flint, comes only from Anatolia.

Traders may have traveled distances of up to 500mi. Because many items, such as textiles and skin products, have not survived, the full extent of the trade network cannot be known.

Clay-using cultures of the Near East
Periods are represented by named archeological sites.

9000–8500 BCE PROTO-NEOLITHIC PERIOD (PRE-POTTERY NEOLITHIC A)
Sites: Jericho, Jordan; Mureybet, Syria

First evidence of handmade bricks

8500–7000 BCE ACERAMIC NEOLITHIC PERIOD (PRE-POTTERY NEOLITHIC B)
Sites: Jericho, Jordan; Ain Ghazal, Jordan; Beidha, Jordan; Mureybet, Syria; Tell Abu Hureyra, Syria; Chayonu, Turkey; Jarmo, Iraq; Ganj Dareh, Iran

Use of handmade bricks; rectangular houses with plaster floors; clay modeling of animal and human figurines

8000 BCE
Site: Mureybet, Syria

First evidence of fired pottery

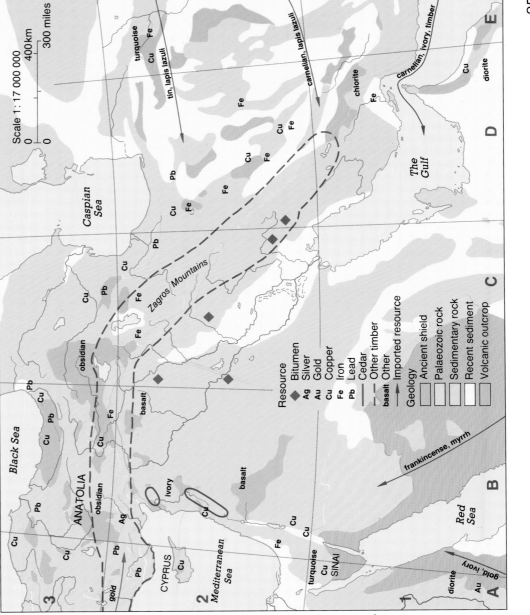

Scale 1 : 17 000 000

0   400km
0   300 miles

Resource
◆ Bitumen
Ag Silver
Au Gold
Cu Copper
Fe Iron
Pb Lead
— Cedar
— Other timber
— basalt Other
→ Imported resource

Geology
Ancient shield
Palaeozoic rock
Sedimentary rock
Recent sediment
Volcanic outcrop

Black Sea
Caspian Sea
ANATOLIA
CYPRUS
Mediterranean Sea
Red Sea
SINAI
The Gulf
Zagros Mountains

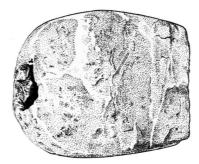

Above A pot made from a type of lime plaster called white ware, developed in about 8000 BCE. Before people used pottery, containers were made from many different materials.

Right Raw materials and trade. The Zagros Mountains were rich in minerals and wood. Copper came from Sinai, while Anatolia supplied obsidian, timber, and metals. Mesopotamia had deposits of bitumen but otherwise lacked any resources. Tracing a metal or a stone to its source helps us to understand the development of trade.

THE ART OF POTTERY

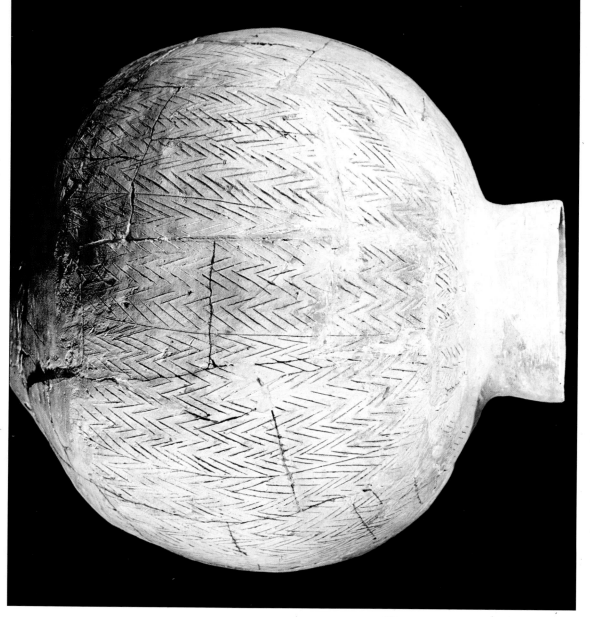

AFTER 8000 BCE PEOPLE WHO LIVED IN villages began using pottery throughout the Near East. Complete pottery vessels are sometimes found at archeological sites, but usually only hundreds of sherds (pottery fragments) are discovered. Pottery was cheap, especially if it was locally produced, so if a vessel broke, it was just thrown away.

Baked clay, from which pottery is made, is almost indestructible and can survive all sorts of weather conditions. Even if a city was burned, the pottery fragments would survive. Many sites are covered with a layer of potsherds that are left after the wind and rain have washed away the surface soil. These remains help archeologists learn about a site.

WHAT POTTERY TELLS US ABOUT A SITE

Pottery can be used to date a site, especially before the invention of writing. In different periods and at different places, pottery was produced in various ways and decorated with particular designs. From the range of sherds they collect at a site, archeologists can work out when people lived there.

Similar pottery styles found at a number of sites in a region show that people lived in these places at about the same time. Different types of pottery tell us about changes in the settlement of a region over hundreds or thousands of years. Where imported pottery (brought in by trade) is found, we can sometimes work out the links between different groups of people.

Left This early, handmade pottery container from about 6500 BCE is crudely made and only lightly fired. It is porous and could not be used to store liquids. The herringbone pattern on its surface was made using a sharp tool.

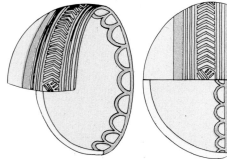

Above Pottery vessels found in an excavation are drawn in crosssection so that archeologists can compare the pottery types from different sites. The left-hand side shows the outside of the bowl and the right-hand side the inside. The drawing is made to scale and shows any decoration.

Left Some styles of pottery were decorated to a high artistic standard. The bowl on the left shows four ibexes (mountain goats) arranged in a cross pattern. It dates from about 5000 BCE, and the style is called Samarra. The beautiful multicolored plate on the right is from the Halaf period (6000–5400 BCE). This fine pottery was only matched by the much later red-and-black Greek Attic ware.

HOW POTTERY WAS MADE

Pottery is made basically from clay, often mixed with an ingredient called a temper. Tempers vary from sand or plant matter to hair. Materials that are naturally present in some clays, such as mica (a mineral), often look like tempers that people have added.

Pottery can be made in a number of ways. Early vessels were hand-made. Pottery could also be molded in different types of forms. The potter's wheel was invented in about 4500 BCE. Pottery made on a wheel often has recognizable marks that show this.

Firing (oven-baking the pottery hard) is also important. Different temperatures and firing times produce different results. The amount of oxygen in a kiln (pottery oven), can change the color of a vessel from red to black.

The surface areas of the pottery could be treated in different ways. They might be given a thin coat of liquid clay called a slip. After 1500 BCE glazes (glass-like finishes) were also used. Patterns and designs might be painted on or incised (marked) into the clay using a stick or another tool. Some pots were polished to a shiny finish, a process called burnishing.

Right A potter is making a vessel using a series of coils which he will build up, either smoothing them with his hand or finishing them on a potter's wheel. Most pottery was wheel-made, but some vessels were molded. Bowls were made by pressing clay into forms. They were very common and may have been used to bake bread. Nearby are the pots which the potter has made and decorated. Some designs were marked on the surface using a sharp instrument or a stick. Others were painted with vegetable dyes. Finally, the vessels would be fired hard in a pottery kiln (oven).

FIRST CIVILIZATION (7000–4000 BCE)

P OTTERY USE WAS WIDESPREAD IN THE
Near East by 7000 BCE. Distinctive pottery
types emerged at different sites, after which
the cultures have been named. Most settlements
were in the dry-farming zone of rainfall (10in a
year). Over the next 3,000 years village life became
more organized, and fields were irrigated.

EARLY POTTERY CULTURES

The rectangular mud-brick houses in the village at
Tell Hassuna, in northern Iraq, had several rooms
and courtyards. Pottery was fired in large domed
kilns. Clay spindle whorls indicate that wool was
woven here. Obsidian, turquoise, and seashells
found here point to trade with Anatolia and Sinai.

The Samarra and Choga Mami cultures spread
south from Hassuna. Early farmers relied on
rainfall to sustain their crops, but in these areas the
rainfall alone was not enough. At Choga Mami,
water channels show that irrigation was used to
bring water to the fields.

Below *Ubaid pottery was
decorated with dark painted
patterns on a pale background.*

Right *An Ubaid female
figurine from Ur with an
unusual "lizard-like" head.*

HALAF CULTURE

The Hassuna culture was replaced by the Halaf, named after the site on the Khabur river in Syria. People here lived in domed mud-brick round huts called *tholoi*. The Halaf culture produced beautifully painted pottery. By 5500 BCE the northern Halaf culture came into contact with the Ubaid culture.

UBAID CULTURE

The Ubaid culture developed in the south of Mesopotamia and lasted for over 1,000 years. At Eridu in Sumer, a series of temples were built, possibly to the water god Enki. A cemetery was found containing 200 rectangular mud-brick graves. The houses had a central room flanked by two rows of rooms. The distinctively painted pottery from the Late Ubaid has been found in Saudi Arabia, Bahrain, and Qatar. This shows that there was already appreciable trade with The Gulf region.

Right Finely carved jars and a bowl made from alabaster (a compound of gypsum and water). They were found in graves from the Samarran period excavated at Tell al-Sawwan in central Iraq.

Pottery cultures, 7000–4000 BCE
Cultures are represented by named archeological sites.

7000 BCE PROTO-HASSUNA

6800 BCE HASSUNA
Sites: Hassuna, Iraq; Tell Umm Dabaghiyeh, Iraq

6500 BCE SAMARRA
Sites: Tell al-Sawwan, Iraq; Choga Mami, Iraq

6000 BCE HALAF (EARLY)
Sites: Tell Halaf, Syria; Arpachiyeh, Iraq; Yarim Tepe, Iraq

5900 BCE UBAID (EARLY)
Site: Tell Halaf, Syria

5400 BCE UBAID (LATE) *Site:* Eridu, Iraq

Below Early pottery cultures, 7000–5400 BCE. In about 6000 BCE the Hassuna culture overlapped the Samarra culture. About 1,000 years later the Halaf culture spread through the Zagros Mountains to northern Syria. The Ubaid culture developed in Sumer in southern Mesopotamia.

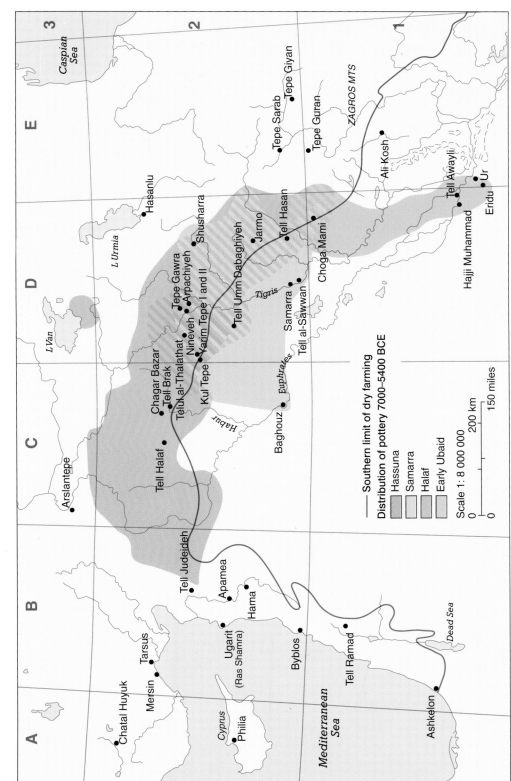

Scale 1: 8 000 000

0   200 km
0   150 miles

— Southern limit of dry farming

Distribution of pottery 7000–5400 BCE
- Hassuna
- Samarra
- Halaf
- Early Ubaid

TELL MADHHUR

TELL MADHHUR IS IN EASTERN IRAQ, NOT far from the Iranian border. It was excavated as part of a project to study sites that have now been flooded by the construction of a nearby dam.

The buildings at Tell Madhhur were made from mud baked hard in the sun. In the center of the mound was a large house built in about 4000 BCE during the Late Ubaid period. The walls of the house, almost 7ft high, had remained standing because, although the house had been burned, people had deliberately filled it in with soil. Everyday household items such as pottery vessels, clay spindle whorls, and stone hoes had also survived.

Right *A bird's-eye view of the Tell Madhhur house, showing its layout. The hearth where the food was cooked is in the central room. Side rooms were used for storing vegetables and grain. The house was single-story. A ramp led up to the roof, where people may have slept, as they still do today in the Near East during hot summer nights. Several families probably shared the house.*

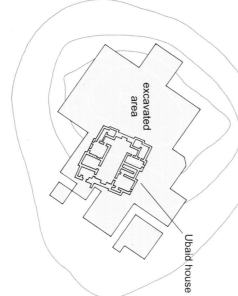

excavated area

Ubaid house

contours at 20in intervals

30

Left *The Tell Madhhur site. Much of the area was buried under thick layers of silt that had been deposited in the valley since Ubaid times. The Ubaid village had about 12 houses, all built in the same tripartite style.*

Tell
• Madhhur

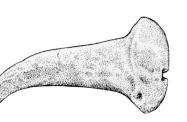

Right A baked-clay pestle shaped like a bent nail. In the Late Ubaid period many tools were made out of baked clay. They were as strong as stone utensils. Other baked-clay items found at Tell Madhhur include grindstones and spindle whorls.

"TRIPARTITE" ARCHITECTURE

The house had a long central room, the main living area, flanked on each side by several smaller rooms. This was the usual way that Ubaid houses were built. The design is called "tripartite" because the house had three areas (the central room and the two sides). Tripartite houses have been found at Ubaid sites such as Tepe Gawra in northern Iraq.

The style also seems to have been used for temples. Three temples at Tepe Gawra were built according to a tripartite plan, as were others in the south, at Eridu and Uruk. Where this style first came from is not known, but it may have come as the result of trade or contact with people further south. It became the main form for Near Eastern temple architecture. People built tripartite temples for almost 2,000 years, from southern Mesopotamia to northern Syria.

Above Not all the tools found at Tell Madhhur were baked clay. These stone hoes were made of chipped flint. They would have been attached to a wooden handle by bitumen and a cord. Only stone and clay products survived the fire.

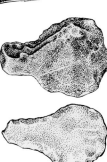

Above Among the 78 pottery items found in the house was this small painted cup or bowl. Pottery of all shapes and sizes was found. Some of the grain-storage jars were enormous and could hold as much as 24 gallons.

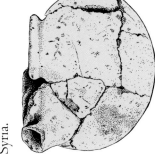

Above A spouted jar, for storing and pouring liquids, was found in the kitchen. Similar vessels have been found at other sites. Most pots in the house were hand-made, but some may have been finished on a wheel.

In ancient times many daily tasks were carried out in the same area, and rooms were multi-purpose.

1. Main living area, with the hearth where food was cooked and bread was baked. In winter people slept here.
2. Adjacent kitchen area where people are grinding grain to make bread. Other food preparation took place.
3. Side storage room where grain is sieved.
4. Stairs leading to the roof of the single-story house where people slept in summer.
5. Storage rooms for food.
6. Entrance to house.
7. Open drainage channel.

BIRTH OF THE CITY (4000–3000 BCE)

T HE FIRST CITIES DEVELOPED IN SOUTHERN Mesopotamia in about 4000 BCE. Much earlier, Jericho and Çatal Hüyük had shown some of the features of cities – including walls and closely spaced housing. But these early sites were unique, and the "urban revolution" only began later in the Uruk period.

The change from village to city life took place between 4300 and 3450 BCE. Larger numbers of people began living more closely together, and many of them ceased to be farmers. Religious centers such as temples began to be built. In the Early and Middle Uruk periods, the northern region around Nippur was well populated. In the Late Uruk period, most settlements were in southern Mesopotamia. This movement of people may have been caused by the Euphrates river changing its course. In the following Jamdar Nasr and Early Dynastic periods, many thousands of people lived in the city of Uruk and its surrounding areas.

SPECIALIZED LABOR

Large urban populations involved a very different social organization from that of villages. Many people became specialists in crafts and trades instead of farmers. In the Uruk period, large temples were built. Artistic activity increased throughout the Near East, reaching Egypt in about 3000 BCE. Traders were active, importing lapis lazuli, a blue semiprecious stone, over 1,250mi from Afghanistan. Copper and its alloys became common and may have been worked by professional smiths. A metal industry was developing, using gold, silver, copper, lead, and iron.

Farmers were using the ox-plow by 4000 BCE, and their produce may have been carried to cities in carts pulled by oxen or, in the marshes of southern Mesopotamia, by boat. Records made by scribes of the goods received at Uruk are the earliest known written documents.

Right The Arabs who live in the marshes of southern Iraq today use boats for transport. The boats are built from reeds, waterproofed with bitumen. They are similar in design to boats found at the Royal Cemetery at Ur (about 2600 BCE). Clay models of boats were found in an Ubaid grave at Eridu from about 4000 BCE.

Below Towns of the Late Uruk period. When the Euphrates changed its course, many settlements were abandoned in the north. Large numbers of people moved south, settling nearer Uruk, which was already a big city.

Right Towns of the Early–Middle Uruk period. More than half the population of southern Mesopotamia lived in the fertile alluvial plains to the north and east of and around Nippur. The Euphrates and Tigris rivers were then joined farther upstream.

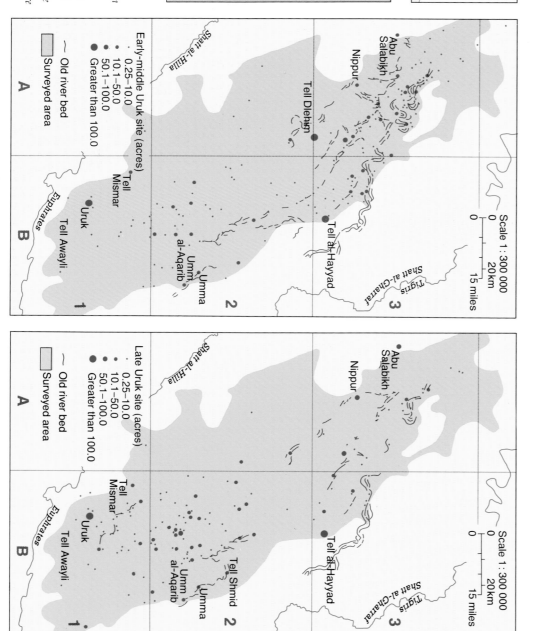

Early-middle Uruk site (acres)
• 0.25–10.0
● 10.1–50.0
● 50.1–100.0
● Greater than 100.0
〜 Old river bed
Surveyed area

Abu Salabikh
Nippur
Tell Dlehm
Tell ai-Hayyad
Tell Mismar
Uruk
Tell Awayli
Umm al-Aqarib
Umma

Shatt al-Hilla
Euphrates
Tigris Shatt al-Gharraf

Scale 1:300 000
0   20km
0   15 miles

A   B
1   2   3

Late Uruk site (acres)
• 0.25–10.0
● 10.1–50.0
● 50.1–100.0
● Greater than 100.0
〜 Old river bed
Surveyed area

Abu Salabikh
Nippur
Tell ai-Hayyad
Tell Mismar
Tell Shmid
Uruk
Tell Awayli
Umm al-Aqarib
Umma

Shatt al-Hilla
Euphrates
Tigris Shatt al-Gharraf

Scale 1:300 000
0   20km
0   15 miles

A   B
1   2   3

MESOPOTAMIAN SITES

URUK

U RUK WAS ONE OF THE MIGHTIEST CITIES IN
Sumer, southern Mesopotamia, between
4000 BCE and 3000 BCE. The site is near
modern Warka, 156mi southeast of Baghdad. The
Bible mentions Uruk twice: in Genesis, ch. 10 (as
Erech), and in Ezra, ch. 4.

Uruk probably developed from two Ubaid
settlements, Kullaba and Eanna, where there were
temples to the sky god, Anu, and the goddess of
love, Inanna. In about 3000 BCE the two sites
joined together to form a single city. Uruk covered
an area of 1,000 acres and was surrounded by a
wall 6mi long.

Gilgamesh, the hero of the great Sumerian
story *The Epic of Gilgamesh*, was said to be a king
of Uruk.

TEMPLES AND THEIR TREASURES

An important religious site grew up at Uruk,
centered on the two temples of Anu and Inanna.
The tripartite temples were built on a terrace

*Left This statuette of an
unknown ruler of Uruk dates
from the late 4th millennium
BCE. Such figures were placed
in temples as a sign of the
ruler's devotion to the gods.*

*Below A priestly procession is
entering the temple precinct at
Uruk. The mighty columns of
the monumental entrance are
over 6ft in diameter and are
decorated with colored cones
stuck into the plaster. A sheep
and piles of dates are being
brought to the goddess Inanna.
The temples were much involved
in the way food production was
organized.*

taking up one-third of the city. Parts of the temple were decorated with geometric designs made from thousands of stone or clay cones painted red, black, and white. Inside were a stepped altar and a central table for burnt offerings. Staircases on the side led to the roof where particular prayers had to be uttered.

Treasures from the temples were as splendid as the buildings themselves. A white marble woman's face was found in a pit near the Inanna temple. The mask is almost life-size and probably had semiprecious stones (lapis lazuli) inlaid in the eye sockets. This superb work of art, known as the "Mona Lisa of Uruk," may have represented Inanna herself.

An alabaster vessel over 3ft high was found at the Uruk temple site. The Warka vase, with three bands of carving, shows the earliest known religious scene in Mesopotamia. In the top band, food is being offered to Inanna. In the middle a procession of naked men (possibly priests) carry baskets of produce. The bottom band has a frieze of sheep and grain-heads. The carvings seem to represent a thanksgiving festival for good harvests.

Left This Warka vase (c. 3000 BCE) was one of a pair found in the temple treasury at Uruk. The detail (**Above**) shows the goddess Inanna, or her priestess, standing in front of long red poles (top center). She receives a gift from a man in a long gown, perhaps the king of Uruk. The many offerings behind her include two vases like the Warka vase. Two priestly figures stand on the sheep's back.

CYLINDER SEALS

CYLINDER SEALS ARE SMALL CYLINDER-shaped objects on which a scene or a design is carved. The seal's carving leaves a "print" when it is rolled out on clay. The scene can be reproduced as many times as the cylinder seal is turned. Cylinder seals average about 1in high and 2/3in in diameter. They were usually made out of stone, but metal, ivory, wood, bone, shell, and baked clay were also used. Being small, they were easy to carry.

HISTORY OF CYLINDER SEALS

The earliest cylinder seals to be found are from Uruk and are dated about 3500 BCE. The idea spread quickly throughout the Near East and as far as Egypt. Cylinder seals were valuable, and were those made from semiprecious stone, and were probably passed down from one generation to the next. After about 3,000 years, people gradually stopped using the seals because alphabets came into use.

Left and right A limestone cylinder seal and a drawing of the impression that was made in clay. The metal mount at the top is fashioned as a bull, echoing the cattle design on the seal print.

Below The mudhif or guest-house of the Marsh Arabs of southern Iraq is still built of reeds today. Its ancient design is shown on cylinder seals from Late Uruk times (3000 BCE).

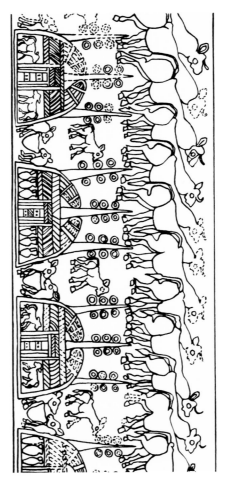

Below Many cylinder seals were made of luxury stones, such as lapis lazuli, and worn by their owners as jewelry. The seals were usually pierced lengthwise so that they could be worn on a pin or a piece of string, or mounted on a swivel.

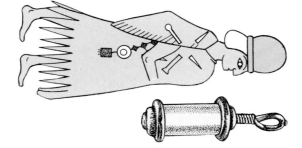

Right The man on the left of the picture has cut off small lumps of clay, which he is flattening on to pots. He then gives them to the overseer, who rolls a cylinder seal over them to produce a pattern or impression. When they have set, the seals are attached with rope to the necks of the jars.

Below Cylinder seals were made by cutting hard stone with flint or copper tools. When the cylinder had been shaped, the artist would carve the scene or design. Cylinders were pierced with a hand bore to make the hole through which a pin or wire was threaded.

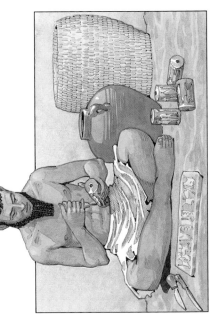

WHAT CYLINDER SEALS WERE USED FOR

Cylinder seals were used to mark the ownership of property. In the case of a storage jar, impressions on a lump of clay would be attached to a string which tied down the cover.

Cylinder seals were often used with cuneiform (wedge-shaped) writing, which had also developed at Uruk. Legal and commercial documents were written on clay tablets and often show the impression of a cylinder seal engraved with the owner's name.

The cuneiform inscriptions on cylinder seals tell us the names that people had and about family history. Their carved designs often show scenes from daily life or highlight the role of the king. Many scenes also illustrate the gods, religious worship, and Mesopotamian mythological stories. People may have believed that their seals had magical properties.

The clay impressions left by the seals provide valuable archeological evidence too. At Jamdat Nasr, north of Uruk, a cylinder-seal print on a clay tablet bore the symbols of the gods of many towns. Similar clay sealings have been found at Ur in Sumer, perhaps suggesting that there was a league of city-states.

Left and below A series of cylinder seal "prints" from different periods. They show animals and mythological creatures. Some of the prints have cuneiform (wedge-shaped writing) inscriptions.

THE EARLIEST KNOWN WRITING COMES from Uruk and has been dated to about 3300 BCE. It took the form of "word-pictures" drawn with a pointed instrument (a stylus) on to tablets of damp clay. Much later the complete system had more than 700 signs. The tablets measured about 2in wide and were ¾in thick. Each word-picture represented an object: a bull's head meant cattle, an ear of barley meant grain.

Writing developed at Uruk as a convenient way to keep records of produce and accounts of trade. The first tablets that can be read record the transfer of food and other goods including beer. Writing was used first for business and later for literature.

Above A hollow clay sphere and tokens. The markings on the sphere may show the number and range of tokens once enclosed inside. Many such spheres with tokens have been found in Elam (southwest Iran) and Sumer.

Right A clay tablet from Uruk inscribed with a very early form of writing. The signs in the lower line may be read as "priest," "prince," and "great." The wedges may be numbers.

Above A cuneiform letter and its envelope. Clay tablets were often put inside such containers. To make sure nobody changed the contents of the letter, identical writing was put on the outside too.

Above Cuneiform signs were made by pressing a sharpened reed stylus into clay (right). Most tablets were square, but round ones (left) were used for scribes to learn to write on. It took many years to learn the hundreds of signs.

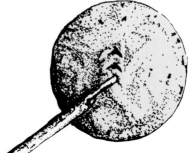

TOKENS FOR TRADE

Tokens had developed much earlier than writing. Clay tokens came in various shapes and sizes, perhaps representing different objects. A cone may have meant a bag of wheat, for example, and a disk, a sheep. Later, the symbol for a sheep became a cross inside a circle.

Tokens were placed inside hollow clay spheres (balls) that were then sealed. If one person sent six sheep to another, the sender would put six tokens in the sphere. When the sheep arrived the receiving person would break open the sphere and count the tokens. Then the person would know whether the correct number of sheep had arrived.

The number of tokens also began to be marked on the surface of the sphere. This was probably how writing on clay tablets began.

Right In the temple warehouse, jars of barley and dates are being stacked by laborers. A temple scribe records amounts of produce on a tablet, while a senior official checks the tablets that are drying on the table. Many early cuneiform documents are lists of food received by temples.

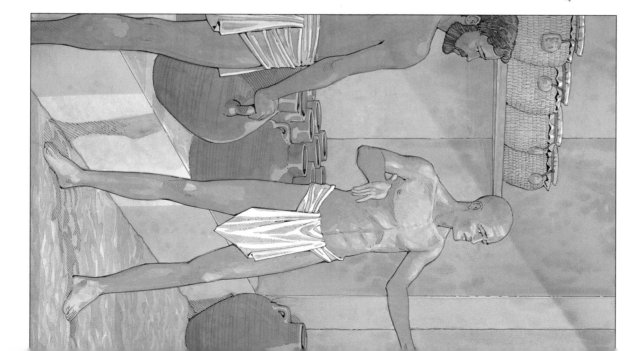

PICTOGRAPHIC SIGN c. 3100 BCE								
INTERPRETATION								
star	?sun over horizon	?stream	ear of barley	bull's head	bowl	head + bowl	lower leg	?shrouded body
CUNEIFORM SIGN c. 2400 BCE								
CUNEIFORM SIGN c. 700 BCE (turned through 90°)								
PHONETIC VALUE*								
dingir, an	u_4, ud	a	še	gu_4	nig_2, ninda	ku_2	du, gin, gub	lu_2
MEANING								
god, sky	day, sun	water, seed, son	barley	ox	food, bread	to eat	to walk, to stand	man

* Some signs have more than one phonetic value and some sounds are represented by more than one sign. U_4 means the fourth sign with the phonetic value u.

Right The main stages in the development of the cuneiform script. The later signs have changed greatly from the original word-pictures. This is partly because by 700 BCE the signs had been turned 90 degrees (a right angle). The signs went through many changes of both position and meaning. The Assyrians had a vocabulary of 570 signs of which 300 were often used.

CUNEIFORM SCRIPT

The word-pictures written on the tablets at Uruk developed into the script we now call cuneiform. It was a complicated process.

The pictures began to represent ideas and became "ideographs." For example, a bull's head might also mean strength, and the sign of a leg might mean both a person and also to walk. Later the signs became "phonograms," representing sounds as well as the meaning of a picture. The sign of a bull's head now equaled the sound or syllable (a unit of pronunciation of a word) "gu."

Cuneiform (from the Latin *cuneus* = wedge) was a syllabic script with hundreds of wedge-shaped signs that developed from the original pictures.

WHO USED CUNEIFORM?

Cuneiform was used by many different peoples during its 3,000-year history. The Sumerians were the earliest to write in cuneiform. The Assyrians adopted the script in about 2300 BCE, and it was used by the Babylonians, the Elamites in nearby Iran, the Hittites, the Hurrians, and the Urartu who lived in Anatolia. Cuneiform also appears in the Levant.

Other scripts, such as hieroglyphics (a form of picture-writing), were known in the Near East, but cuneiform was the language of politics until the 5th century BCE. It died out in the face of a language that emerged in Syria in about 900 BCE: Aramaic – with only 22 letters – was much easier and quicker to write.

Cuneiform continued to be used by some peoples until the 1st century CE but its 900 signs were reduced to about half that number over time.

STATES IN CONFLICT (3000–2350 BCE)

WHEN THE EARLY DYNASTIC I PERIOD replaced the Uruk culture in about 3000 BCE, Sumer became a land of city-states. Each state consisted of a city and its lands. There were few physical boundaries in southern Mesopotamia besides the water channels, and city-states fought wars with each other – though they remained mostly independent. The first kings came to power at this time.

THE CITY-STATE AND ITS LEADERS

The center of economic wealth in the city-state was the temple. As the home of the patron god or goddess, it was the city's main feature, owned large areas of land and employed many people. The chief priest was called en or "lord."

The cities had governors called ensis. Decisions were made by the free male citizens, probably those who owned land, in a form of democracy. There

was an upper house of "elders," probably distinguished citizens, and a lower house of "men," perhaps the other landowners.

In times of crisis, the assembly would elect a leader, called a lugal. He was the commander in battles with other city-states. He acted as a judge in disputes and later carried out rituals such as blessing the harvests. He lived in a "great house" or egal, a word that came to mean palace.

The lugal or "great man" began to rival the temple in power and wealth. At some point, the position of leader became permanent. Instead of being elected, the lugal became a hereditary king. Kings saw themselves as chosen by a "council of the gods" – which met only at the city of Nippur – to carry out the gods' will. Because of this the Sumerian kings eagerly contributed to the building and maintenance of the religious buildings in the city.

Above One of more than a dozen known copies of the Sumerian King List. The original, now lost, was written in about 2100 BCE.

Left A stone wall-plaque from Girsu, in present-day Iraq. Ur-Nanshe, the ruler of Lagash (about 2480 BCE), one of the Sumerian city-states, is shown carrying a basket of bricks on his head. He is acting in his role as the builder of the city and is watched by a female figure who could be a priestess. In the lower part he is seated on his throne with a cup in his hand. The plaque is inscribed in cuneiform, and the hole indicates that it may have been mounted on a pole.

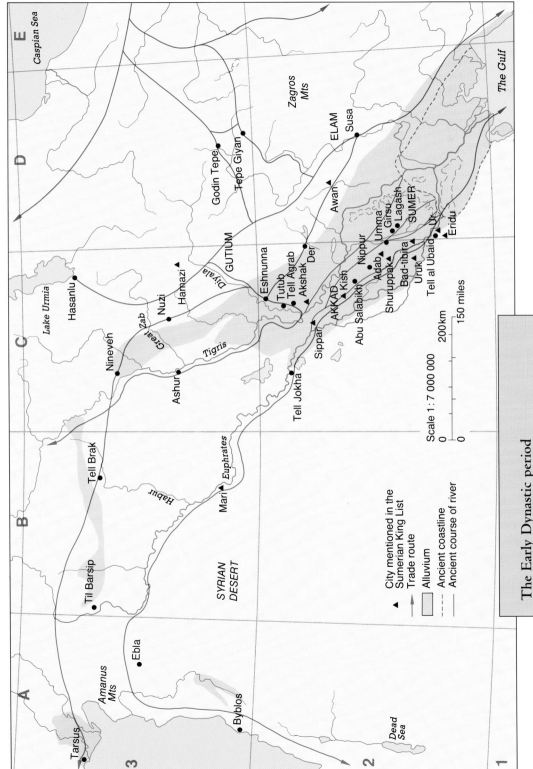

Above Cities in the Sumerian King List. Southern Mesopotamia was divided into two regions. Sumer in the south stretched from Eridu, which was once on The Gulf, to Nippur. The Sumerian King List listed the names of the rulers of the cities of Sumer and the length of their reigns. Reigns were often listed as being very long, even thousands of years. The King List was written to reinforce the idea that kings were linked closely to the gods, who gave assent to their rule. Although not all the facts it states are true, the King List can help us to understand history.

THE SUMERIAN KING LIST

The Sumerian King List is an ancient cuneiform record of royal rulers. At least 12 copies have been found in Babylonia and at Susa and Nineveh. It lists all the kings of the Early Dynastic period, many of whom are mentioned in other cuneiform inscriptions. Although the King List places the kings one after the other, they often ruled at the same time at different city-states.

SUMERIAN INFLUENCE

Sumer was divided into a number of small city-states. Its political influence was weak, but Sumerian culture spread throughout the Near East. Sumerian-style statues were found at Ashur. The city of Mari in eastern Syria had strong links with Mesopotamia. At Ebla, in western Syria, 8,000 clay tablets were found written in a Sumerian cuneiform script.

The Early Dynastic period

Sites: Eshnunna (Tell Asmar), Iraq; Tutub (Khafaje), Iraq

3000–2750 BCE EARLY DYNASTIC I
2750–2650 BCE EARLY DYNASTIC II
2650–2350 BCE EARLY DYNASTIC III

Ensis of Lagash (2570–2342 BCE)
The ensis of Lagash were not included in the Sumerian King List. Unlike kings, they were not said to have received their position from the gods.

c. 2570 BCE En-Hegal
c. 2550 BCE Lugal-sha-engur
2494–2465 BCE Ur-Nanshe
2464–2455 BCE Akurgal
2454–2425 BCE E-ana-tum
2424–2405 BCE En-ana-tuma I
2404–2375 BCE En-temena
2374–2365 BCE En-ana-tuma II
2364–2359 BCE En-entar-zi
2358–2352 BCE Lugal-anda
2351–2342 BCE Uru-ku-gina

Scale 1:7 000 000

0   200km

0   150 miles

Key:
▲ City mentioned in the Sumerian King List
Trade route
Alluvium
Ancient coastline
Ancient course of river

Caspian Sea
Zagros Mts
ELAM
Susa
Awan
Godin Tepe
Tepe Giyan
GUTIUM
Eshnunna
Tutub
Tell Agrab
Akshak
Der
Nippur
Adab
Umma
Girsu
Lagash
SUMER
Ur
Eridu
Tell al Ubaid
Uruk
Bad-tibira
Shuruppak
Kish
AKKAD
Abu Salabikh
Sippar
Tell Jokha
Hamazi
Diyala
Nuzi
Great Zab
Tigris
Nineveh
Ashur
Hasanlu
Lake Urmia
Mari
Habur
Euphrates
Tell Brak
Til Barsip
Ebla
Byblos
Tarsus
Amanus Mts
SYRIAN DESERT
Dead Sea
The Gulf

41

MESOPOTAMIAN SITES

NIPPUR

LOCATED 100MI SOUTH OF BAGHDAD, Nippur is a huge *tell* 66ft high and covering an area of 750 acres. People lived at Nippur for more than 5,000 years, until the 9th century CE. In the Early Dynastic period, the lands of Sumer and Akkad met at this city.

Enlil, the lord of the air, was the main Sumerian god. His temple at Nippur was the most important shrine in Sumer. Sumerians believed that it was at Nippur that the gods met in an assembly to elect kings.

Kings of the Third Dynasty of Ur may have lived at Nippur in about 2000 BCE, but the city was never the capital of a dynasty. Rulers of other cities thought that control of Nippur, with its religious importance, gave them the right to rule all of Sumer and Akkad.

During the reign of Ur-Nammu, (2112–2095 BCE), the first ziggurats, the high temple platforms, were constructed in Mesopotamia. The ziggurat at Nippur was built in about 2100 BCE. At the top of this vast tiered structure was Enlil's temple, which was called the *ekur* or "mountain house." It became the most important shrine (holy place) in Mesopotamia. Near the ziggurat was the temple of Inanna, the Mesopotamian goddess of love and war.

The remains of the ziggurat are still very visible, and 100 years ago excavators from the University of Pennsylvania built a dig-house on the top of the mound to protect themselves from the local warring Arab tribes. Since then the site has been much excavated, particularly by archeologists from the University of Chicago.

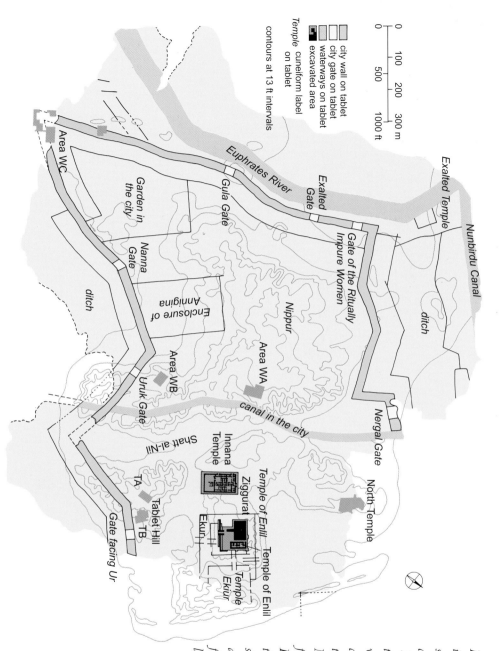

Left *The site of Nippur, including features from a unique scale drawing of the city on a cuneiform tablet dated about 1300 BCE. The tablet shows the temple of Enlil, the city walls, the gates and the main canal. Thousands of cuneiform tablets have been found at Nippur, where there was a famous scribal school. Excavations at the south end of the site have found where the sharp ends of the wall join. In ancient times the Euphrates flowed by the eastern walls, but later the river changed course.*

Nippur

EBLA

Tell Mardikh was identified as the ancient city of Ebla in 1968. Located in Syria, south of Aleppo, people lived at Ebla for over 3,500 years, until 800 CE. Its most important period was from 2500 BCE to 1500 BCE.

Eight thousand cuneiform texts were discovered at Ebla. They came from the library of what is called "Palace G." Most of the clay tablets were written in Eblaite, a previously unknown local language that is closely related to the language of Akkad. Many of the texts discuss administrative matters. The king was extremely wealthy, owning 80,000 sheep and receiving income of 11lb of gold and 1,100lb of silver each year.

Below The ancient city of Ebla. The city covered an area of around 120 acres and had an enormous royal complex at its heart.

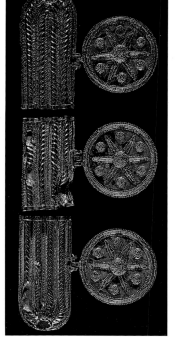

Right A human-headed golden bull with a stone beard, found in Palace G at Ebla. The figure may be linked to worship of the sun god Shamash. It is Sumerian in style. Later, huge human-headed bulls guarded the entrances to Assyrian palaces.

Below A gold necklace, dated to about 1750 BCE, found in a tomb beneath Ebla's Western Palace. The decoration on the disks was made with tiny gold granules, and the three-section band was made by "coiling." These techniques were developed in Sumer.

Below Ebla's archive room. From traces left behind after the burning of this room, the original shelving system can be worked out. When the room was discovered, the clay tablets lay where they fell when the wooden shelves collapsed in the city's destruction. Many of the tablets were badly smashed and must be painstakingly pieced together.

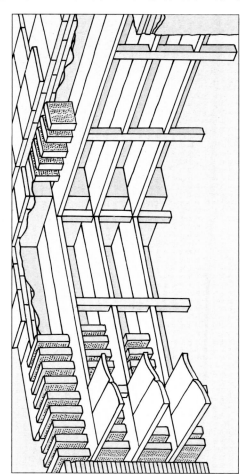

EBLA AND SUMER

Ebla had many links with Sumer. Some texts were written in both Eblaite and Sumerian. Delicate gold jewelry found in Palace G had been made using techniques developed in Sumer's Early Dynastic period. A limestone inlay was decorated with battle scenes in typical Sumerian style.

Ebla was a thriving kingdom, at its wealthiest between 2400 BCE and 2250 BCE, when the Early Dynastic period ended and the Akkadian rulers came to power. The city's huge royal complex contained a palace, buildings for administration and storage, and workshops. Ebla traded far and wide – from nearby Carchemish to central Anatolia, Ashur in northern Mesopotamia, and Afghanistan. After being attacked by the Mesopotamian king Naram-Sin (2254–2218 BCE) the city never recovered its economic prosperity.

MESOPOTAMIAN SITES

UR

THE ANCIENT CITY OF UR IS IN SOUTHERN Iraq. It was founded during the Ubaid period in about 4000 BCE when people also first settled in Sumer. Ur was near the Euphrates river, and some of the city's earliest remains were covered with heavy silt from it. This may be evidence of a terrible flood, memories of which were handed down and recorded in the Bible (Genesis, chs 6–8).

Genesis, ch. 11, claimed Ur as the home of the Hebrew patriarch Abraham. Ur was also a port for trade with The Gulf until 1700 BCE. The main temple was dedicated to the moon god Nanna. The city was abandoned in about 300 BCE, probably due to floods.

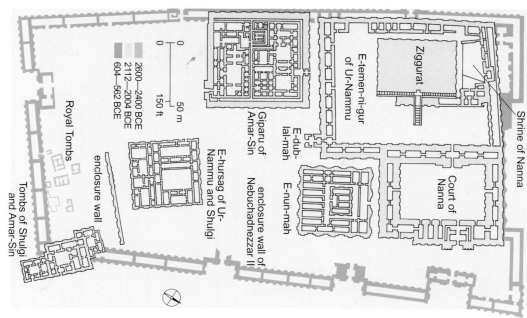

Ziggurat

E-temen-ni-gur of Ur-Nammu

Shrine of Nanna

Court of Nanna

E-dub-lal-mah

E-nun-mah

Giparu of Amar-Sin

enclosure wall of Nebuchadnezzar II

E-hursag of Ur-Nammu and Shulgi

enclosure wall

Royal Tombs

Tombs of Shulgi and Amar-Sin

0   50 m
0   150 ft

2600—2400 BCE
2112—2004 BCE
604—562 BCE

Above Two lyres as they were found in the tomb of Queen Puabi. In the dust can be seen the cow's head made of gold and lapis lazuli that was attached to one of these musical instruments.

Left The sacred enclosure with the temple and the ziggurat of Nanna, the moon god. It was built by the kings of the Third Dynasty of Ur (2112–2004 BCE). Ur-Nammu, Shulgi, and Amar-Sin also seem to have lived and been buried here. The royal tombs were inside the walls.

Below Gaming boards similar to this one were found in the royal tombs. They were made from pieces of shell, bone, lapis lazuli, and red limestone set into various patterns. Two sets of seven counters were used to play the game, but the exact rules are unknown.

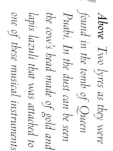

Above An exquisitely worked gold dagger (with lapis lazuli handle) and sheath. The Sumerian goldsmiths were masters of their craft. The sheath was decorated in fine granules of gold.

THE ROYAL CEMETERY AT UR

Excavations in the 1920s uncovered more than 1,000 graves at Ur from the end of the Early Dynastic period (2600–2400 BCE). In some of the tombs spectacular treasures were found, including the so-called "Standard of Ur," a delicately inlaid box with a banquet scene on one side and a war procession on the other. It is now in the British Museum.

Inscriptions identify the royal graves of King Meskalamdug and Queens Puabi and Ninbanda. Mass burials suggest that human sacrifice took place – some kings and queens were buried with their servants, who seem to have died by drinking poison or taking a drug.

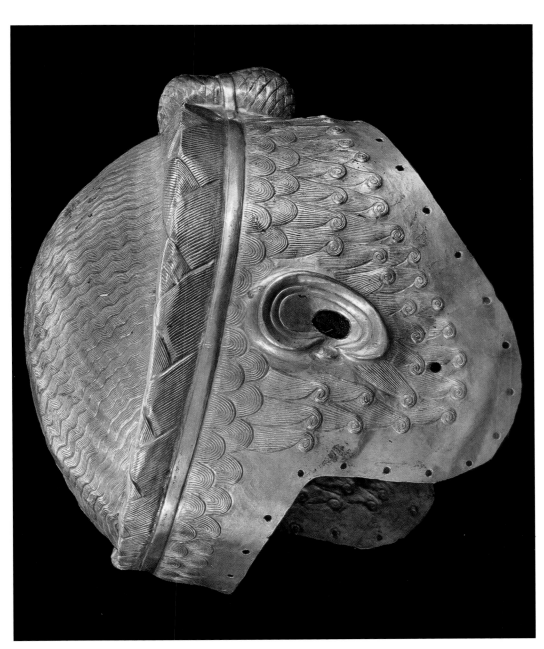

Above Reconstructed wooden sledge from the royal tomb of Queen Puabi. Two oxen were found still attached to the sledge in the tomb. The reins passed through a silver ring decorated with a donkey made from electrum (a gold/silver alloy).

Above A stone weight shaped like a duck, found at Ur. The inscription gives its weight as "5 minas for Nanna." A mina weighed about 1lb.

Right A superb electrum helmet from the tomb of King Meskalamdug. The Sumerians could dissolve silver from the surface of the alloy so that it would look like gold. The finely fashioned hair is held in place by a diadem suggesting a royal owner.

ZIGGURATS

L OOKING VERY IMPRESSIVE AGAINST THE FLAT
Mesopotamian landscape, pyramid-shaped
ziggurats symbolized sacred mountains and
were first built in about 2000 BCE. People had
already built temples on platforms at Eridu in the
Ubaid period, and ziggurats were similar religious
buildings. They appeared with the revival of
Sumerian rule after the dynasty of Akkad
(2334–2154 BCE). King Ur-Nammu of the Third
Dynasty of Ur constructed ziggurats at Ur, Eridu,
Uruk, and Nippur.

DESIGN OF THE ZIGGURAT AT UR

The ziggurat at Ur had a rectangular base with
three staircases that met at right angles and went up
to two more stages to reach the high temple. The
ziggurat core was made of mud-bricks, but burned
bricks with a bitumen mortar were used for the
outside. Many bricks were stamped with Ur-
Nammu's name. Drains carried off the water from
the upper parts.

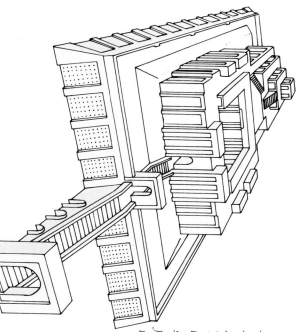

*Left The ziggurat at Tell al-
Rimah was built by Shamshi-
Adad I in about 1800 BCE.
The ziggurat was part of the
temple building, and the upper
shrine was probably reached
from the roof of the courtyard
temple.*

THE ZIGGURAT OF BABYLON

Ziggurats were built throughout southern and northern Mesopotamia and also in Elam. When Babylon became the center of religious worship, its ziggurat became more famous than the one at Ur. This ziggurat was probably built on the remains of an earlier one. It stood for 1,000 years until Sennacherib demolished it in 689 BCE. Dedicated to the god Marduk, the ziggurat became identified with the biblical tower of Babel (Genesis, ch. 11).

Herodotus, the Greek historian, described the ziggurat at Babylon as having six levels crowned by a temple. Its dimensions were also given in a Babylonian clay tablet. The ziggurat was called Etemenanki, which means "the temple of the foundation of heaven and earth."

Below Building a ziggurat involved hundreds of laborers. Some carry mud-bricks, which are being made nearby. Other laborers carry reeds that will be woven into matting to be placed between the layers of bricks.

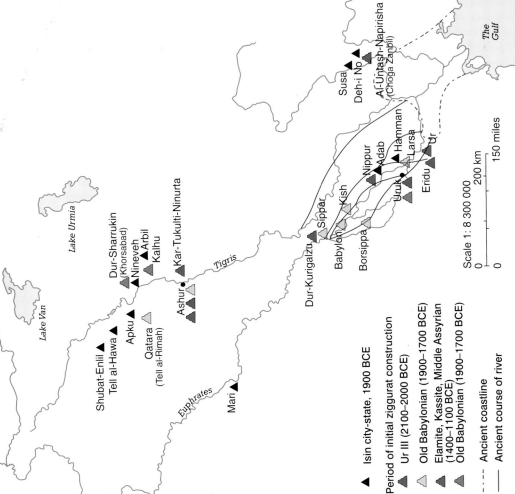

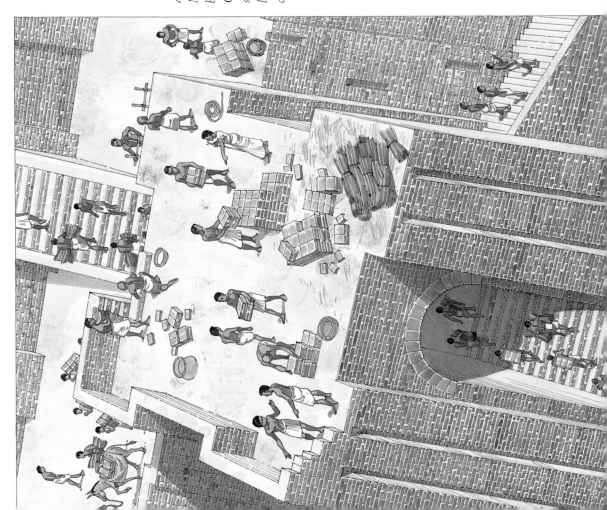

▲ Isin city-state, 1900 BCE

Period of initial ziggurat construction

◢ Ur III (2100–2000 BCE)

◁ Old Babylonian (1900–1700 BCE)

◣ Elamite, Kassite, Middle Assyrian (1400–1100 BCE)

◢ Old Babylonian (1900–1700 BCE)

---- Ancient coastline

— Ancient course of river

Scale 1 : 8 300 000

0   200 km
0   150 miles

Above Ziggurats of Mesopotamia. Ziggurats have been excavated at 16 sites. Others are known from the shape of the mound or from literature. Dur-Sharrukin was one of the first excavated.

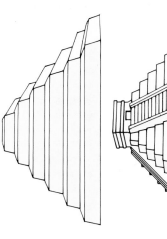
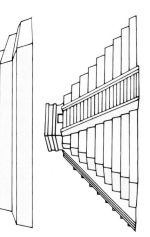

Below Ziggurats look like the stepped pyramids in Egypt (top), which were tombs. Stepped temples are found in Central America (bottom), but there was no contact with Mesopotamia.

Lake Van
Lake Urmia

Shubat-Enlil ▲
Tell al-Hawa ▲
Apku ▲
Qatara ◁
(Tell al-Rimah)

Dur-Sharrukin ▲
(Khorsabad)
Nineveh ▲
Arbil ▲
Kalhu ▲
Ashur ◢
Kar-Tukulti-Ninurta ▲

Tigris

Euphrates

Mari ▲

Dur-Kurigalzu ◢
Sippar ◢
Babylon ◢
Kish ◢
Borsippa ◢
Nippur ▲
Adab ▲
Uruk ◣
Hamman ▲
Larsa ◢
Ur ◢
Eridu ◣

Susa ▲
Deh-i No ▲
Al-Untash-Napirisha ▲
(Choga Zanbil)

The Gulf

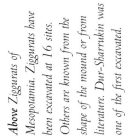

A CCORDING TO MESOPOTAMIAN RELIGION, human beings were created to serve the gods. Each city had a patron god, and these gods lived in images in the temples dedicated to them. The priests and other people who worked at the temples were their servants. Kings were thought to be appointed by the will of the gods.

MESOPOTAMIAN GODS

Anu, the sky god, was the chief Sumerian god. He reigned over the heavens and lived in the uppermost region which was called "the sky of Anu." Anu's city was Uruk, which also housed the famous Eanna temple complex of Inanna, goddess of love and war. Enlil, the "lord of the wind," whose city was Nippur, was the son of Anu. He replaced his father as the main god. Enki, god of living water, had his temple at Eridu. Ur was the city of Nanna, the moon god. Temples at Larsa and Sippar were built for the sun god Utu.

By 2000 BCE, the Sumerian gods became combined with the Akkadian gods and took their names. Inanna became Ishtar. Shamash, which literally meant "sun," replaced Utu. Nanna was now called Sin. In Babylonian times, Marduk became the chief god, with his temple at Babylon.

Above Priests slaughtering a ram. Animal sacrifices were common and could involve large numbers of sheep. The intestines would be examined for omens about the future.

Right Drawings of seal impressions in clay, found at Ashur. The dog was the symbol of the goddess Gula. The goat-fish was linked with Ea, god of waters.

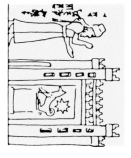

Left A group of Sumerian statues from Eshnunna. They are not gods but represent worshipers and were placed in the temples to pray for the life of the person who gave them. The hands are clasped in prayer. Some of the eyes, inlaid with bitumen and shell, are still intact. Each person was believed to have a special god or goddess who would protect them from demons.

IMAGES OF THE GODS AND DEMONS

The Mesopotamians thought that their gods looked and behaved like people, though they had supernatural powers. A very large number of images of gods and goddesses have been found, from statues to wall plaques. Cylinder seals and other pieces of art show gods and goddesses with human bodies. The gods were shown with beards. To signal that they were different from people, images of the gods and goddesses always included a distinctive multi-tiered horned crown or helmet and a seven-petaled rosette engraved near the head.

Gods and goddesses also had their own symbols. The crescent and circle represented Sin, the moon god. The star was Ishtar's sign. Sometimes the gods held their symbols in their hands. At other times the divine symbols sprouted from their shoulders. The images of the gods and goddesses often changed throughout Mesopotamian history.

Besides the gods, people in the Near East believed in supernatural spirits and demons, both good and bad. Many of these took half-human and half-animal forms. Some demons were thought to cause diseases and other misfortunes, which superstitious people took complicated precautions to avoid.

Above *Ur-Nammu, king of Ur between 2112 and 2095 BCE, makes a libation (drink offering) to the moon god Sin. Sin is seated on a throne, holding in his hand a rod, a ring and possibly a necklace. Water, beer, oil, wine, and blood were used for libations.*

Right *A bronze statue of the king of the evil wind demons, Pazuzu. He is shown with grotesque face, four wings, bird's legs, animal paws and a scorpion's tail. Demons such as Pazuzu were not always evil and sometimes protected people from other demons!*

PART TWO

KINGDOMS AND EMPIRES

Above A cuneiform tablet from the royal library at Nineveh, recording observations of the stars and planets. Assyrian kings employed expert astrologers.

Right Detail from the "war" side of the "Standard of Ur," found in the Royal Cemetery at Ur. It shows the victorious troops of Ur, on foot or in chariots. Four mules pull the empty chariot (top left) of the king (top right) who holds a mace in his hand as a symbol of kingship.

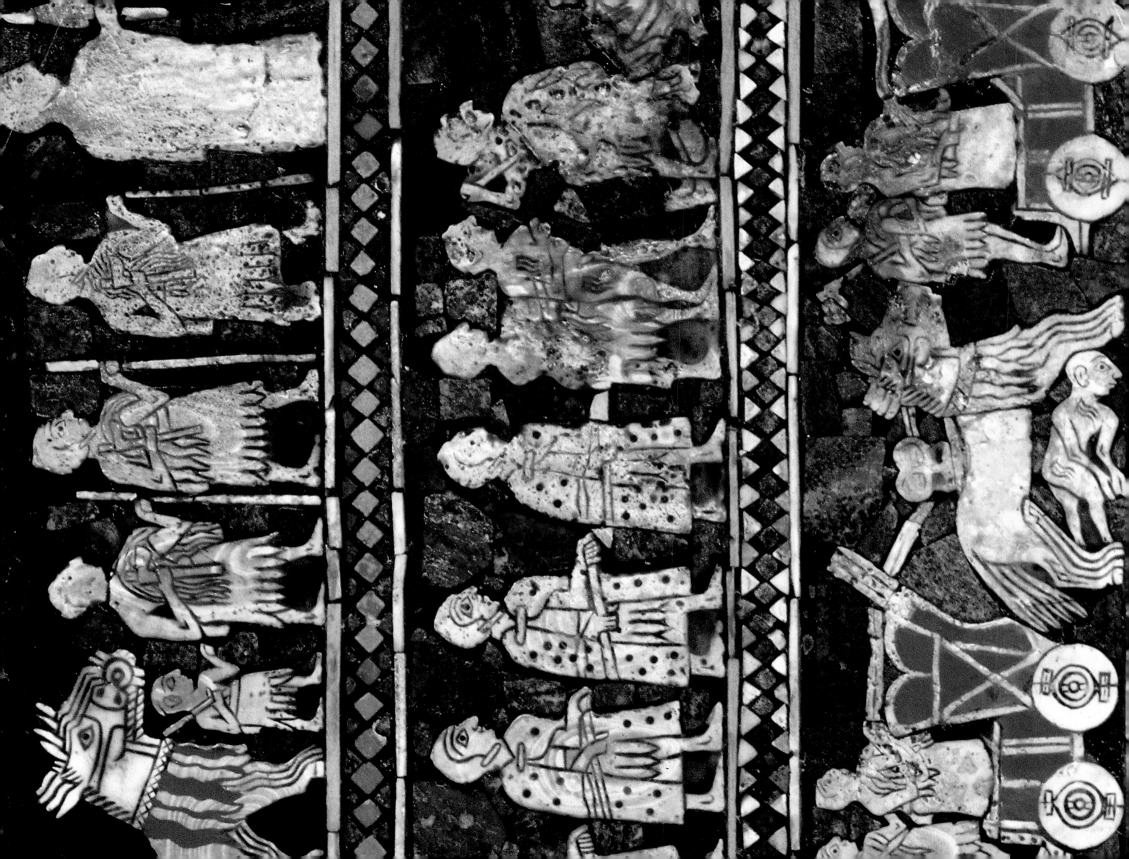

KINGS OF AGADE (2350–2000 BCE)

MESOPOTAMIA BECAME UNITED WHEN Sargon of Akkad conquered both the northern and southern regions of Mesopotamia. The Akkadian language was now spoken rather than Sumerian, and Mesopotamian rule extended throughout the Near East.

SARGON OF AGADE

Sargon was the first king of the dynasty of Agade and ruled for 56 years. His name in Akkadian meant "the true king," but his origins were humble. The Sumerian King List states that his father was a date-grower, and another account says that he was a gardener favored by the goddess Ishtar. He grew to become the royal cup-bearer at the court of Kish.

Sargon built a new capital city at Agade, probably near Babylon. He conquered the city-states of Uruk, Ur, Umma, and Lagash in southern Mesopotamia, and he was also called the King of Kish and King of the Land.

Below *The kings of Agade conquered an empire that stretched from the Mediterranean to modern Iran. Sargon claimed that he ruled the whole world "from the sunrise to the sunset." This boast could have been a later invention. From their widespread territories, the kings of Agade obtained such raw materials as wood from Lebanon and silver from Anatolia.*

SARGON'S SONS

Rimush and Manishtushu, Sargon's sons, continued their father's military campaigns. They took Akkadian rule as far north as Ashur and Nineveh and also east into the Elamite territories. Talking about his conquests of the distant regions Anshan and Sherihum, now in Iran, Manishtushu said: "It is absolutely true!"

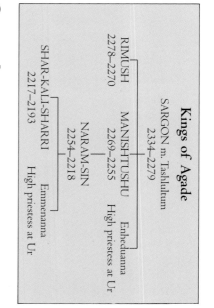

Kings of Agade

SARGON m. Tashlultum
2334–2279

RIMUSH   MANISHTUSHU   Enheduanna
2278–2270   2269–2255   High priestess at Ur

                NARAM-SIN   Emmenanna
                2254–2218   High priestess at Ur

SHAR-KALI-SHARRI
2217–2193

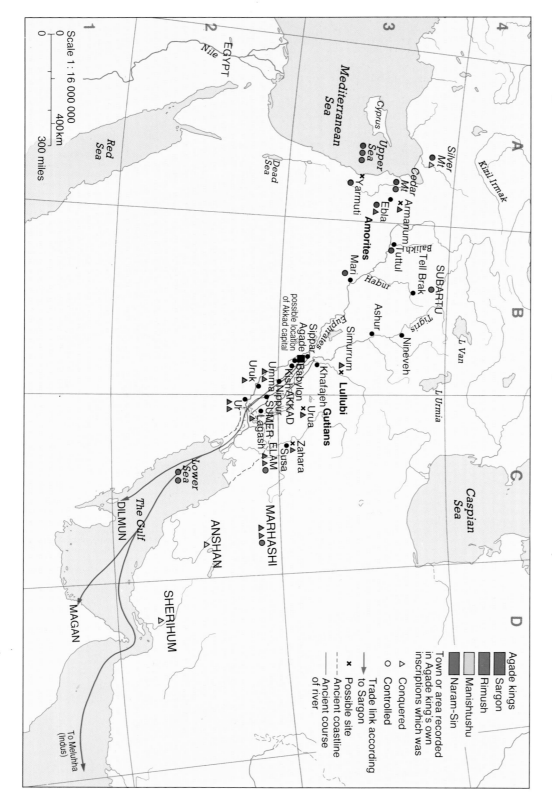

Scale 1 : 16 000 000

0 ——— 400km
0 ——— 300 miles

A
B
C
D

Mediterranean Sea

EGYPT
Nile
Red Sea
Dead Sea
Cyprus
Upper Sea
Kizil Irmak

Silver Mt
Cedar Mt
×Yarmuti
Armanum
Ebla ×
Tuttul
Balikh
Tell Brak
Mari
Habur
Ashur
Nineveh
L Van
L Urmia
SUBARTU

Amorites

Euphrates
Tigris

Simurrum ×
Sippar
Agade
Babylon
Kish AKKAD ×
Umma
Urua
Nippur
Uruk
SUMER
Lagash
Ur
Khafajeh
Lullubi
Gutians
ELAM
Zahara ×
Susa
Caspian Sea

possible location
of Akkad capital

Lower Sea
DILMUN
The Gulf
MAGAN
ANSHAN
SHERIHUM
MARHASHI
To Meluhha
(Indus)

Town or area recorded
in Agade king's own
inscriptions which was

△ Conquered
○ Controlled

→ Trade link according
   to Sargon
× Possible site

---- Ancient coastline
---- Ancient course
      of river

Agade kings		
	Sargon	
	Rimush	
	Manishtushu	
	Naram-Sin	

NARAM-SIN

Naram-Sin, Sargon's grandson, ruled for 37 years and called himself King of the Universe. His empire extended from Susa in the east to Ebla on the Mediterranean coast. He claimed to be a god, making people address him as "god of Agade," and inscriptions show his name marked with the sign that was used to indicate gods. Naram-Sin was followed by his son, Shar-kali-sharri, who reigned for 17 years. But the empire of Agade began to collapse because of internal problems and pressure from the Gutians, who came from the Zagros Mountains. The city of Agade was sacked and has never been found.

THE THIRD DYNASTY OF UR

With the downfall of the Akkadian empire, Sumerian rule revived once more. At Ur, King Ur-Nammu built the famous ziggurat as well as other temples and a palace. Ur-Nammu's power was concentrated in southern Mesopotamia, for he also controlled Eridu and Uruk and erected buildings at Nippur and Larsa. One of his sons married a daughter of the king of Mari, linking the two nations.

Shulgi, Ur-Nammu's son, reigned for 47 years after his father's death. Like Naram-Sin he also claimed he was a god. Shulgi carried on the building work begun by his father and expanded the kingdom eastwards and northwards to Ashur and Susa. He introduced many reforms during his reign, making the governors (*ensis*) and military commanders (*shagins*) report directly to him. Shulgi controlled the temple lands, reorganized the system of weights, introduced a new calendar, established a code of law, and imposed new taxes. In just one year alone 28,000 cattle and 350,000 sheep passed through Puzrish-Dagan, a redistribution center for taxes located a few miles south of Nippur.

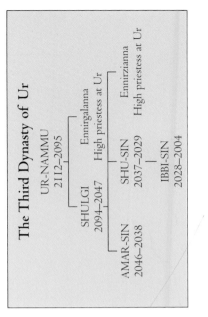

The Third Dynasty of Ur

```
UR-NAMMU
2112–2095

        SHULGI        Ennirgalanna
        2094–2047     High priestess at Ur

AMAR-SIN        SHU-SIN        Ennirzianna
2046–2038       2037–2029      High priestess at Ur

                        IBBI-SIN
                        2028–2004
```

Right *A limestone statue of Gudea, the ruler of Lagash, who wears a fur headdress. He is holding a vase from which flow two streams of living water, symbolized by the fish.*

Below *This superb life-size head was made from copper. It is hollow, but the eyes would have been inlaid with stones. The beard, hair, and diadem indicate a king, possibly Sargon or Naram-Sin.*

RIVAL KINGDOMS (2000–1600 BCE)

I N ABOUT 2000 BCE THE THIRD DYNASTY OF Ur broke up into several smaller kingdoms. This marked the end of a united Mesopotamia. The two most important new kingdoms were Isin and Larsa, after which this period in Mesopotamian history has been named. The most famous king was Rim-Sin of Larsa, who reigned from 1822 BCE to 1763 BCE. In 1804 BCE he defeated Uruk and 10 years later he captured Isin.

New peoples arrived in Mesopotamia and settled among the Akkadian and Sumerian communities. The Amorites – nomads from the Arabian desert region who spoke a Semitic language – became powerful in the kingdoms of Babylon, Kish, and Larsa.

Large numbers of Hurrians, who spoke an Indo-European language, came from Anatolia into northern Mesopotamia and western Syria. Texts from Alalakh on the Orontes river in Syria show that almost half the population there had Hurrian names.

Kingdoms of Mesopotamia, 2025–1595 BCE

Selected outstanding kings are listed for each kingdom.

First Dynasty of Isin, 2017–1794 BCE
Isme-Dagan (1953–1935 BCE)
Lipit-Ishtar (1934–1924 BCE)

Larsa Dynasty, 2025–1763 BCE
Rim-Sin I (1822–1763 BCE)

1763 BCE Rim Sin I defeated by Hammurabi, ending the Larsa dynasty

First Dynasty of Babylon, 1894–1595 BCE
Hammurabi (1792–1750 BCE)

Asur
Shamshi-Adad I (c. 1813–1781 BCE)
Ishme-Dagan I (1780–1741 BCE)

Mari
Zimri-Lim (1779–1757 BCE)

1757 BCE Zimri-Lim defeated by Hammurabi, and the kingdom of Mari ends

Below City-states of the Isin and Larsa period. The rival states that followed the Third Dynasty of Ur were often at war with each other. In 1936 BCE Isin was the largest, stretching from The Gulf to Babylon. Twenty-six years later, in 1910 BCE, it included only Nippur. The southern cities of Ur and Eridu were still ruled by Larsa in 1802 BCE (right), while in the north Babylon had become a major kingdom.

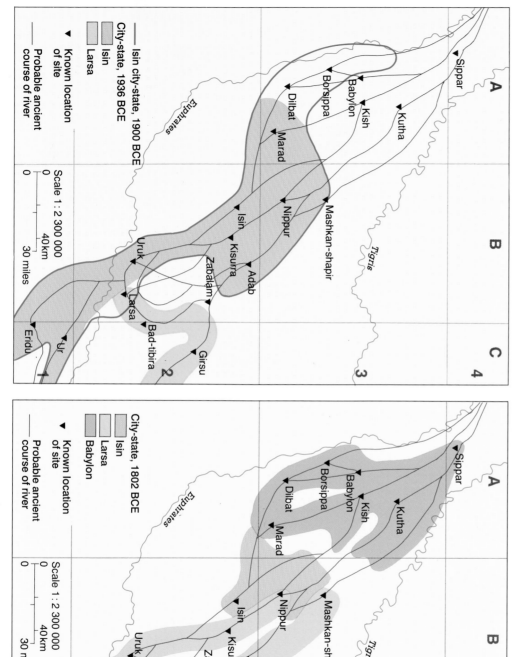

Isin city-state, 1936 BCE
City-state, 1900 BCE
Isin
Larsa

▶ Known location of site
— Probable ancient course of river

Scale 1 : 2 300 000
0   40km
0   30 miles

Euphrates

Sippar · Borsippa · Babylon · Kish · Kutha · Dilbat · Marad · Mashkan-shapir · Isin · Nippur · Kisurra · Adab · Zabalam · Uruk · Larsa · Bad-tibira · Girsu · Eridu · Ur

Tigris

A B C
1 2 3 4

City-state, 1802 BCE
Isin
Larsa
Babylon

▶ Known location of site
— Probable ancient course of river

Scale 1 : 2 300 000
0   40km
0   30 miles

Euphrates

Sippar · Borsippa · Babylon · Kish · Kutha · Dilbat · Marad · Mashkan-shapir · Isin · Nippur · Kisurra · Adab · Zabalam · Uruk · Larsa · Bad-tibira · Girsu · Eridu · Ur

Tigris

A B C
1 2 3 4

TRADE AND CONQUEST IN THE NORTH

The kingdoms of northern Mesopotamia also traded. Ashur, on the river Tigris, was an important center with a large merchant colony dealing in wool, textiles and tin. Tin was used to make bronze, instead of copper, for weapons and other goods. It was mined in Iran and Afghanistan and transported by donkey caravans to Kanesh in central Turkey.

Shamshi-Adad, an Amorite, captured many of the northern kingdoms, including Ashur. His lands stretched from the Zagros Mountains to Mari, on the Euphrates (now in Syria). He claimed to have set up a stele or pillar inscribed with his name "in the country of Laban" (that is, Lebanon). It was the strong personality of Shamshi-Adad which held this Amorite empire together. After his death the reign passed to his two sons who failed to keep control, and so the empire split up. In some places the old kings were restored. In Mari, Zimri-Lim returned to his throne until 1757 BCE, when he was conquered by Hammurabi, king of Babylon.

Left A lapis lazuli necklace from a tomb in Kish. The blue semiprecious stone was mined in Afghanistan. The long brown carnelian beads are typical of the Harappan culture of the Indus valley. These semiprecious stones were imported.

TRADE IN THE SOUTH

The southern Mesopotamian kingdoms competed for the rich trade with The Gulf and beyond. They exported silver, oils, textiles, and barley in exchange for copper, gold, ivory, lapis lazuli, pearls, and other goods. Copper was imported from Magan (modern Oman). Beads found in Mesopotamia show links with the Harappan culture of the Indus valley (Pakistan). Many goods were shipped through Dilmun (probably present-day Bahrain), which was an important trade link between cultures.

Below A donkey caravan at the karum (merchant suburb) outside Kanesh, an important trade center in Anatolia. Donkeys have arrived from Ashur, bringing textiles and tin from Iran. Other donkeys will continue farther west and are being loaded up. One of the merchants is watching his scribe count the goods.

LAW AND SOCIETY

MESOPOTAMIAN KINGS WERE VERY concerned to rule justly. Ur-Nammu of Ur (2112–2095 BCE) wrote the first known law code in the world. His son, Shulgi of Ur, also produced a law code, as did Lipit-Ishar of Isin and Dadusha of Eshnunna. The most famous code to have survived is that of King Hammurabi, who ruled Babylon from 1792 BCE to 1750 BCE.

HAMMURABI'S LAW CODE

Hammurabi's law code is carved on a basalt stele 7½ ft high. The opening words record the king's wish "to cause justice to prevail in the land, to destroy the wicked and the evil, that the strong may not oppress the weak."

The law code may not have been used in courts to decide cases, but the 282 sections cover many subjects, especially property and commercial law. If one person wronged another, financial compensation – in the form of a sum of silver – was often paid, as had been the custom in Sumerian law.

The idea of punishment found in the Old Testament – "Life for life, eye for eye, tooth for tooth, hand for hand, foot for foot" (Deuteronomy, ch. 19, verse 21) – also occurs in Hammurabi's code.

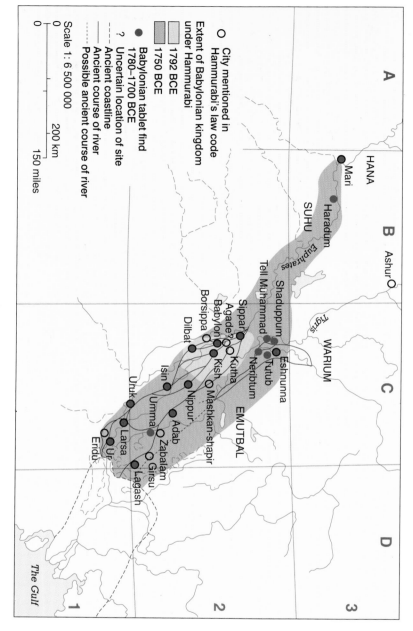

Scale 1: 6 500 000

○ City mentioned in
   Hammurabi's law code
   Extent of Babylonian kingdom
   under Hammurabi
   ▢ 1792 BCE
   ▢ 1750 BCE
   ? Uncertain location of site
   ● Babylonian tablet find
   ● 1780–1700 BCE
   —— Ancient coastline
   —— Ancient course of river
   ······ Possible ancient course of river

A B C D

HANA
Mari
SUHU
Haradum
Euphrates
Ashur ○
Tigris
Shaduppum
Tell Muhammad
WARIUM
Sippar ○
Agade ? ○
Babylon ●
Kish ○
Kutha ○
Neribtum
Tutub
Eshnunna
Borsippa ●
Dilbat ○
Mashkan-shapir
Nippur ○
Isin ●
Umma ○
EMUTBAL
Uruk ○
Adab
Zabalam ○
Larsa ●
Girsu
Lagash ●
Ur ●
Eridu ○

The Gulf

1 2 3

Left This statue, made from diorite, a hard black stone, is thought to be of Hammurabi. He is shown on his law code stele wearing a similar type of headdress. Babylonian kings between 2100 BCE and 1700 BCE wore the same type of royal apparel. The statue was found at Susa, in modern Iran, where it had been taken as war booty in the 12th century BCE.

Left Hammurabi's kingdom. Hammurabi ruled over Mesopotamia only in the second part of his long reign (1792–1750 BCE). He captured Isin and Uruk in 1787 BCE. Later, in 1763 BCE, with the help of the kings of Mari and Eshnunna, he conquered his long-standing rival, Rim-Sin I of Larsa. In 1761 BCE Hammurabi defeated Mari and in 1755 BCE he was victorious over Eshnunna.

BABYLONIAN SOCIETY

Hammurabi's law code divides Babylonian society into three social classes: *awilum* (the Akkadian word meaning "man"), *mushkenum* and *wardum*. The *awilum* were "freemen" who may have been landowners. They may have had to pay taxes and perform military service in the royal army. The *mushkenum* could speak in the assembly of "freemen" but probably did not own property. The *wardum* were slaves. All three classes were, of course, ruled by the king.

When an *awilum* died, his property was divided between his sons. If he fell into debt or could not pay his taxes to the king, he might sell himself, his wife, or his children as slaves.

The king used slaves to build roads, dig canals, and perform other duties. Slaves were expensive to buy, so few were privately owned. Most farms were worked by tenants, who gave a portion of their harvest to the landowner in return for food, animals, and other daily requirements.

PENALTIES UNDER HAMMURABI'S CODE

Hammurabi's law code applied different penalties for the same crime, depending on the social class of the person involved. If the victim was an *awilum*, the person responsible was punished in the same way as they had hurt the victim. Law 196 stated that "If an *awilum* has put out the eye of a *mar-awilum* (the son of an *awilum*), they shall put out his eye". (This was "retributive punishment.")

If the victim was either a *mushkenum* or a *wardum*, then a sum of money would be paid instead. Law 198 states: "If an *awilum* has put out the eye of a *mushkenum* or broken his bone, he shall pay one *mina* of silver."

The idea of retribution – "an eye for an eye" – was not found in Sumerian law and was probably introduced into Mesopotamia by the Amorites.

Right The stele of Hammurabi's law code from about 1760 BCE. The upper part of the basalt pillar shows the king in prayer before the seated Shamash, the sun god and god of justice. Shamash is winged and is also wearing the divine horned crown. He is holding in his right hand a ray of sunlight. The lower part of the stele is inscribed in cuneiform with Hammurabi's 282 laws carved in 49 vertical columns. The Elamites took the stele to Susa in 1159 BCE as war booty from Babylon.

MITTANI AND THE ASSYRIANS

I N NORTHERN MESOPOTAMIA AND THE Levant, the kingdom of Mittani became the major power by about 1500 BCE. The people of Mittani were Hurrians. (The Hurrian language was very different from other Near Eastern tongues.) Their rulers had Indo-European connections and worshiped ancient Indian gods. The Mittanians used a new military weapon: the horse-drawn two-wheeled chariot. Washukanni, their capital city, was probably in present-day northern Syria.

WARFARE WITH EGYPT

Egypt was united by Ahmose, the founder of the 18th dynasty. In this New Kingdom period Egyptian pharaohs conquered much of the Levant and Palestine, with many sites showing signs of massive destruction. Pharaoh Amenophis II (1427–1401 BCE) led an army into Mittanian territory, capturing the city of Qadesh on the Orontes river.

THE AMARNA LETTERS

The only written information about the Mittanians comes from foreign sources. The Amarna letters, a collection of 350 clay tablets, give many details about the government of the Egyptian New Kingdom's territories. They also record diplomatic exchanges between the pharaohs of Egypt and the rulers of independent countries, including Mittani.

Treaties between different states were often cemented through marriage between the rulers' families, and there were many foreign princesses in the harems of the pharaohs. Documents show that royal marriage negotiations were often very complicated and drawnout. Tuthmosis IV (1401–1391 BCE) asked the king of Mittani, Artatama, no less than seven times for the hand of his daughter before his wish was granted. This marriage was probably made in an attempt to block the growing power of the Hittites and the Assyrians.

Below The empire of Mittani in about 1500 BCE. The empire stretched east from Assyria to the Levant. Washukanni, the capital city, has not been positively identified, but may be Tell al-Fakhariyeh in northern Syria. The region around the upper part of the Habur river was the heartland of the empire. Mittanian documents have also been found nearby at Tell Brak.

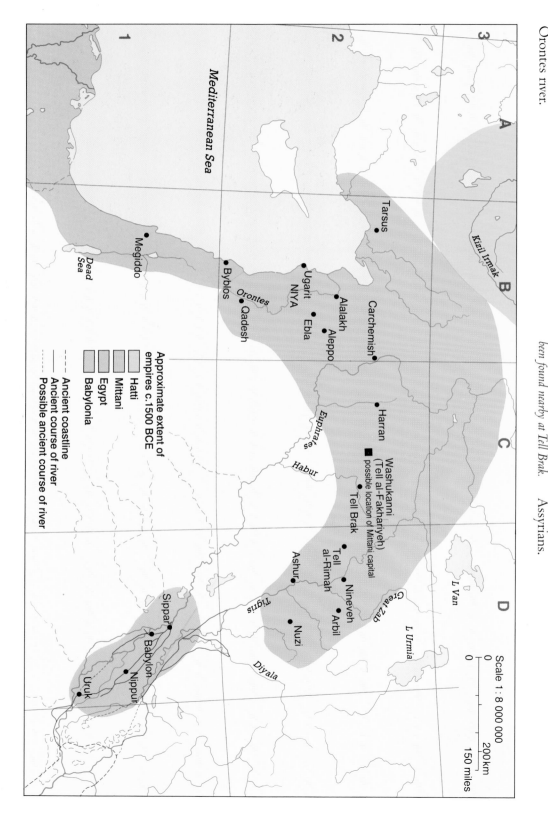

Mediterranean Sea

Dead Sea

Kizil Irmak

Megiddo

Tarsus

Byblos

Ugarit

NIYA

Alalakh

Ebla

Aleppo

Orontes

Qadesh

Carchemish

Harran

Washukanni (Tell al-Fakhariyeh) possible location of Mittani capital

Euphrates

Habur

Tell Brak

Ashur

Tell al-Rimah

Nineveh

Arbil

Nuzi

L Van

L Urmia

Great Zab

Tigris

Diyala

Sippar

Babylon

Nippur

Uruk

Approximate extent of empires c.1500 BCE

Hatti

Mittani

Egypt

Babylonia

Ancient coastline
Ancient course of river
Possible ancient course of river

Scale 1:8 000 000

0   200km
0   150 miles

Above One of the 350 letters from Tell Amarna in central Egypt which record the political history of the pharaohs Amenophis III and Akhenaten. These clay tablets were written in cuneiform, using Akkadian, the international language of the time. Many of the letters describe the situation in Palestine. In the letter shown here, the ruler of Amurru explains why he did not receive the pharaoh's envoy in person.

Above A statue of king Idrimi of Alalakh, in northern Syria, who was a vassal of the Mittanian rulers. The seated king's band on his breast shows his allegiance. Details about his life are given in a cuneiform inscription covering most of his body.

THE HITTITES AND ASSYRIANS

Hattusas in Anatolia was the capital of the Hittites. The Hittites were rivals of the Mittanians for control of their lands, and they ended Hammurabi's dynasty when Mursilis I (1626–1595 BCE) overran Babylon.

The Hittites had peaceful relations with the Egyptian pharaohs. Their king Suppiluliumas I made an alliance with the Assyrian powers and married his daughter to the king of Babylon. His victories in Anatolia, the Levant, and northern Mesopotamia reduced the lands held by Mittani, which had grown weaker.

The Assyrian king Adad-nirari (1305–1274 BCE) captured Washukanni and made its ruler, Shattuara, his vassal (junior ruler). The Mittanian kingdom came to an end when it was annexed by Adad-nirari's son Shalmaneser I (1273–1244 BCE). The Assyrians and the Hittites were now the main powers in Mesopotamia.

59

THE KASSITES (1600–1200 BCE)

THE BABYLONIAN KING LIST RECORDS THAT there were 36 Kassite kings of Babylon, covering a period of several hundred years. After the Hittites conquered the city in 1595 BCE, Babylon was governed by the Kassites for four centuries, from the end of the 15th until the 12th century BCE. The Kassites may have come originally from Central Asia. They did not speak a Semitic language, and only 48 Kassite words have been identified. Some of these are technical terms for horses — and the Kassites were also noted for their horsemanship. When the Kassites first arrived in Babylon they were agricultural workers. Later, even when their kings ruled Babylon, the Kassites do not appear to have been a large group.

DUR-KURIGALZU

The Kassites rebuilt and restored temples at Ur, Uruk, and Isin. But the best-preserved example of their work is at the site of Aqar Quf, near Baghdad, which was called Dur-Kurigalzu. This site was a city built to defend the kingdom against Assyria and Elam. The city was a large one, covering about 495 acres. There was a palace as well as a ziggurat which still stands today at a height of 188ft. Dur-Kurigalzu was a major city, but the Kassites regarded Babylon as the capital of their empire and also its religious and commercial center.

Kassite kings

Kara-indash	c. 1415
Kadashman-Harbe I	
Kurigalzu I	
Kadashman-Enlil I	1374–1360
Burna-Buriash II	1359–1333
Kara-hardash	1333
Nazi-bugash	1333
Kurigalzu II	1332–1308
Nazi-marutrash	1307–1282
Kadashman-Turgu	1281–1264
Kadashman-Enlil II	1263–1255
Kudur-Enlil	1254–1246
Shagarakti-shuriash	1245–1233
Kashtiliash IV	1232–1225
Tukulti-Ninurta	1224–1216
Enlil-nadin-shumi	1224
Kadashman-Harbe II	1223–1222
Adad-shuma-iddina	1221–1216
Adad-shuma-usur	1215–1186
Melishpak	1185–1171
Marduk-apla-iddina I	1170–1158
Zababa-shuma-iddina	1157
Enlil-nadin-ahi	1156–1154

60

The Kassite dynasty, c. 1570–1154 BCE
Selected Kassite kings. (Other rulers from the same period are shown in parentheses.)

c. 1570 BCE Agum II
c. 1510 BCE Burna-Buriash I

c. 1390 BCE Kurigalzu I
(Amenophis III of Egypt)

1359–1333 BCE Burna-Buriash II

1332–1308 BCE Kurigalzu II
(Akhenaten of Egypt)

1263–1255 BCE Kadashman-Enlil II
(Hattusilis III, Hittite king)

1232–1225 BCE Kashtiliash IV
Assyrian king Tukulti-Ninurta sacks Babylon

1170–1158 BCE Marduk-apla-iddina
1156–1154 BCE Enlil-nadin-ahi

Below The Kassite kingdom in the 13th century BCE. This was an empire that covered most of southern Mesopotamia. It bordered Elam in the east, (now modern Iran) and the Assyrian territories in the north. The Elamites overran the Kassite kingdom in the mid-12th century BCE. They took back some of the war booty from Babylon, including Hammurabi's law code stele and Naram-Sin's victory stele, to their capital city Susa. The booty was discovered there in the 19th century by a French expedition.

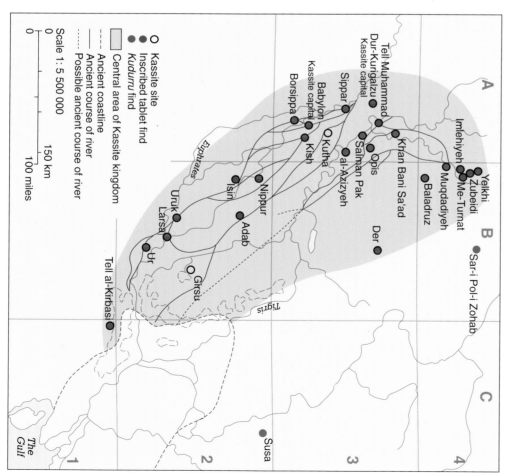

Scale 1 : 5 500 000

○ Kassite site
● Inscribed tablet find
●● *Kudurru* find
▨ Central area of Kassite kingdom
—— Ancient coastline
— Ancient course of river
····· Possible ancient course of river

KASSITE ART AND CULTURE

The Kassites kept the Babylonian way of life, even rebuilding the temples of the Mesopotamian gods who were different from theirs. Their art was lively and realistic, especially when depicting animals. Their scribes left thousands of documents written on tablets.

They were the first people in the Near East to make molded baked bricks to form decorative wall friezes. At the Inanna temple at Uruk, the outer wall shows the gods as humans. Molded baked bricks were used 1,000 years later in the palaces built by Nebuchadrezzar at Babylon and Darius at Susa.

The Kassites also showed skill in carving stone. Boundary stones (*kudurru*) were set up to proclaim when land was given by royal grants. They were often richly decorated with images of beasts symbolizing the gods who were believed to witness such grants.

KASSITE KINGS

Several Kassite kings are named in the Amarna letters. Burna-Buriash II (1359–1333 BCE) is recorded as complaining that the Egyptian delegation who came to collect his daughter and take her to Egypt to be married had only five carriages – not enough for a princess of high rank! The Amarna letters detail the many gifts exchanged between the Kassite king and the Egyptian pharaoh. The Kassite king Kurigalzu I (about 1390) received gold from Egypt.

The most famous king was Kurigalzu II (1332–1308 BCE), who was a successful military leader. He attacked the Elamites and captured Susa, their capital city. Later the tables were turned when the Elamite king Shutruk-Nahhunte attacked the Kassite kingdom. Babylon, the capital, was destroyed and much booty was taken back to Susa. The Kassite period ended in 1154 BCE.

61

Above *Made of limestone, this kudurru or boundary stone is beautifully carved. An inscription in cuneiform (wedge-shaped) script records a grant of land.*

Right *The ziggurat of Dur-Kurigalzu. European travelers thought that the ziggurat was the Tower of Babel. The reed matting that was laid between every seven layers of brick can still be seen. The bottom platform is a modern restoration.*

Below *This painted pottery bead, found at Dur-Kurigalzu, shows the realism of Kassite art. The man's face is painted with red ochre, and his beard and other features are in black.*

EVERYDAY LIFE

B Y 2000 BCE MOST PEOPLE IN THE NEAR
EAST lived in towns and cities that were
protected by walls. Houses were made of
mud-brick and had two stories with flat roofs. The
doors and windows were made from reeds set in
wooden frames. The streets were narrow and
winding, like the old parts of cities in the region
today.

FOOD AND DRINK

Barley was used for bread-flour and for beermaking.
Beer was also brewed from dates, which were an
important source of sugar, as honey was rare. Of
beer it was said, "it makes the liver happy and fills
the heart with joy." People grew onions, garlic, figs,
and pomegranates. Mustard, cress, cumin, and
coriander were used. Sheep, goats, and pigs
provided meat, and people also bred ducks and
geese for food. There were many different types of
fish. Locusts were considered a delicacy.

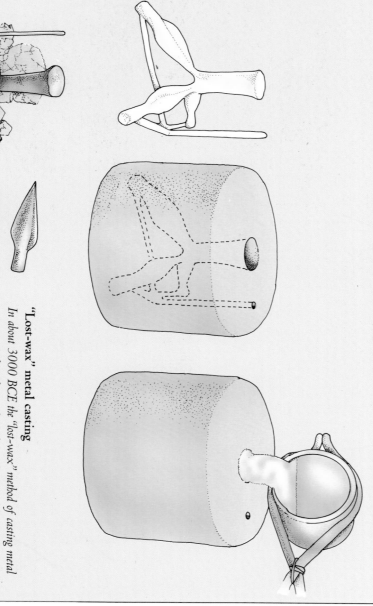

"Lost-wax" metal casting
In about 3000 BCE the "lost-wax" method of casting metal
was invented, replacing the earlier technique of hammering. A
model was made of wax, which was then covered with clay.
When heated, the wax melted and was drained out. Hot liquid
metal was then poured into the clay mold. When the metal became
solid, the clay mold was broken open and the object was taken
out. This method was used for a wide variety of objects, from
arrowheads to life-size sculptures.

CLOTHING AND TEXTILES

Cloth was made from the fleece of sheep, which
was spun on hand-spindles. Spinning and weaving
were done mainly by women, who worked in the
home to provide a source of household income.
Hides of animals were tanned to make leather
goods such as bags and sandals. Men and women
used both soap and cosmetics. They painted the
skin around their eyes with kohl, a metal-based
black paint.

TOWN CRAFTS

There were many different occupations in the
towns. Potters produced a wide range of household
items, from plates and cups to large containers for
storing grain. Carpenters made wooden furniture
and tools, though these were also made from
copper, tin, and bronze. Other craft workers
manufactured metal and glass objects, but these
were luxury items.

Right This 4½ in-high sieve pot
may have been used to strain the
grains when pouring beer, a very
popular drink. Pottery items
made in a wide variety of
shapes and sizes are the most
commonly found objects of
ancient daily life.

Right A Near Eastern street
market. In the shadow of the
ziggurat, traders sell their wares
from small booths. The jars hold
imported olive oil and wine,
while dates and a variety of
spices are also on sale. A temple
official checks the quality of the
food being sold. As coins were
invented only in the 7th century
BCE, payment was made in
corn. This was measured using
standard weights that were often
carved in the shape of animals
or birds, especially ducks.

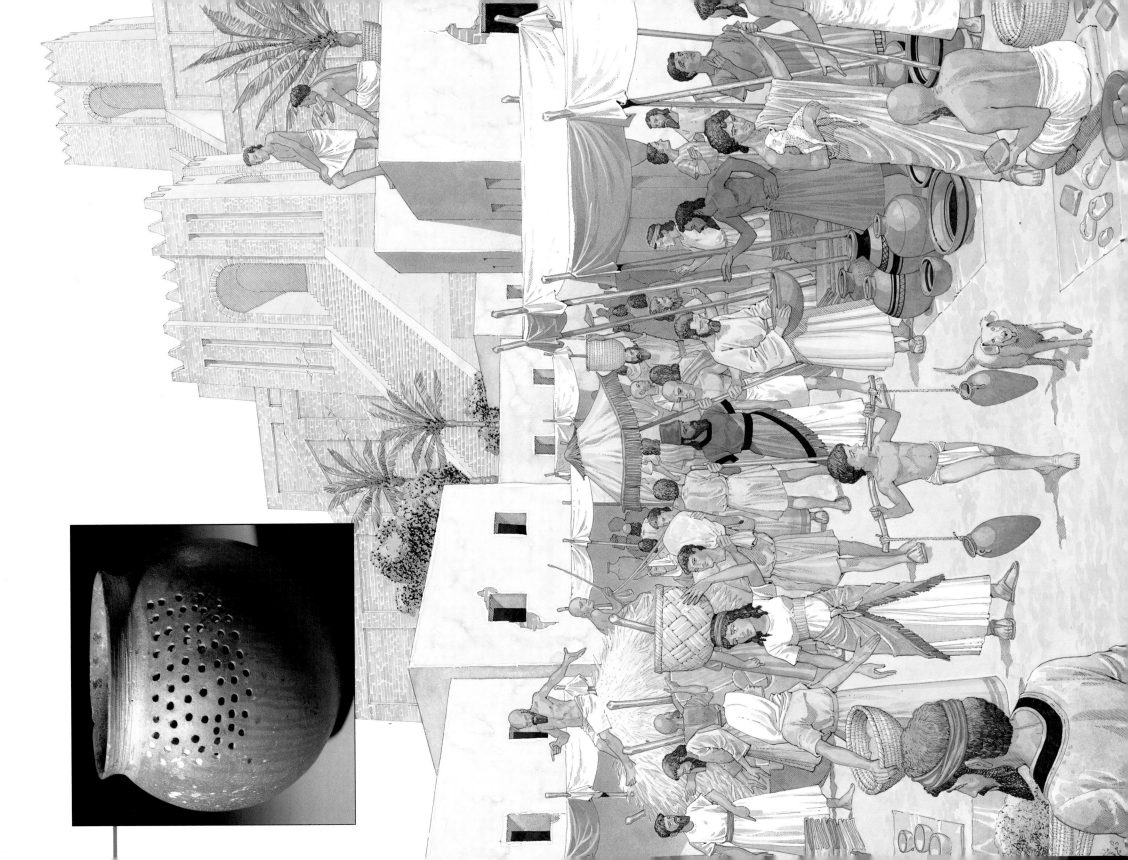

NEW POWERS

I N ABOUT 1200 BCE SMALL GROUPS OF RAIDERS emerged in the Near East and the Levant. The great Hittite empire crumbled, and Egypt was severely shaken. New political forces arose to shape the history of the Near East for the next 1,000 years and more.

THE SEA PEOPLES

Egypt and the Levant were attacked by seafaring raiders known as the "Sea Peoples." Pharaoh Ramesses III (1194–1163 BCE) fought these invaders, who were probably made up of several different tribal groups. The Sea Peoples may have come from the Aegean in the west.

One of the seafaring tribes, driven out of Egypt by Ramesses III, settled on the Mediterranean coastal plains. These people were called the Philistines in the Bible, and their name lives on in the word Palestine. The Philistines adopted much of the local Canaanite culture, but their distinctive decorated pottery shows contact with Mycenaean (Greek) cultures.

BABYLON AND ASSYRIA

Babylon remained under the rule of local kings. Its power grew again briefly under Nebuchadrezzar I (1126–1105 BCE). He plundered the neighboring capital Susa, bringing back to Babylon the statue of Marduk that had been looted by the Elamite king Shutruk-Nahhunte in 1159 BCE.

Assyria became a great power when Tiglath-Pileser I (1115–1077 BCE) expanded its territories as far as the Levant. His campaigns against such peoples as the Ahlamu, or Aramaeans, were recorded in graphic detail on stone carvings at his palace in Nineveh, showing shocking war scenes. Tiglath-Pileser I also hunted wild elephants in northern Syria.

THE ARAMAEANS

The Aramaeans were originally nomads who came from the Syrian desert. They established several small kingdoms in northern Syria and the Levant, blocking Assyria's advance to the Mediterranean. Aramaean power grew, and Adad-apla-iddina (1069–1048 BCE), king of Babylon, was called the "Aramaean usurper." The Aramaeans spoke Aramaic, which replaced Akkadian as the main language of the Near East until Arabic emerged in 700 CE. Some of the letters still survive in modern Armenian and Georgian alphabets.

Above The triumph of the Egyptian pharaoh over his enemies is symbolized in this ivory carving. It shows a lion killing a Nubian (from northeast Africa), against a background of lilies and papyrus flowers.

Below The infantry troops of Tiglath-Pileser I (1115–1077 BCE) are laying siege to a city in Syria. Its gates are firmly shut, but its walls are being breached by a movable wooden siege-engine that is manned from the inside and carries archers on top. The city's defending soldiers have leather-and-wicker shields. Their weapons are made from bronze, although iron was sometimes used at this time.

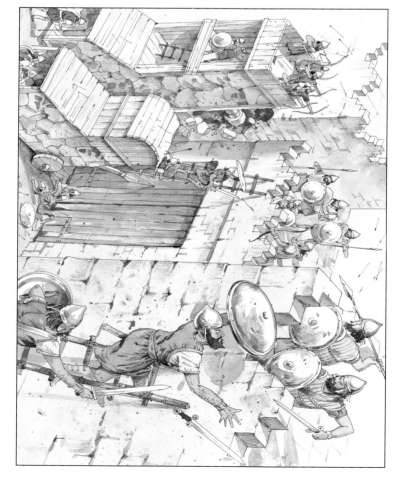

Above Modern Gaza on the coast of Israel. In the 12th and 11th centuries BCE, it was the center of Philistine power and a gateway to Egypt along the coast. In the Bible, it is where Samson met his death.

Left A decorated pot from Ugarit, Syria. It dates from the 13th century BCE. Similar vessels have been found in Cyprus.

Left Female clay figurines, dating from about 900 BCE, found near the coast of the Levant inhabited by the Philistines. They represent the goddess Astarte and emphasize fertility.

Right The Assyrian empire of Tiglath-Pileser I. The empire extended to the western Euphrates and was not troubled by the Sea Peoples who overran Egypt, the Levant, and Anatolia.

Kings of Egypt, Assyria and Babylonia

Egypt
1194–1163 BCE Pharaoh Ramesses III

Assyria
1115–1066 BCE Tiglath-Pileser I

Babylonia (Second Dynasty of Isin)
1126–1105 BCE Nebuchadrezzar I
1069–1048 BCE Adad-apla-iddina

Elam
c. 1159 BCE Shutruk-Nahhunte

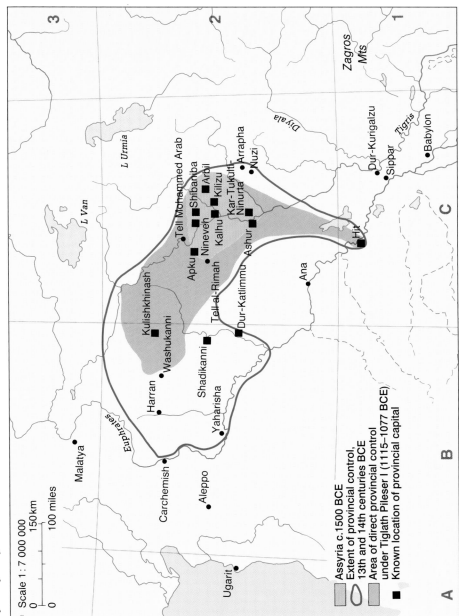

Scale 1 : 7 000 000

Assyria c.1500 BCE

Extent of provincial control,
13th and 14th centuries BCE

Area of direct provincial control
under Tiglath Pileser I (1115–1077 BCE)

■ Known location of provincial capital

Malatya

Carchemish

Aleppo

Ugarit

Harran

Kulishkhinash

Washukanni ■

Shadikanni ■

Yaharisha

Tell-al-Rimah ■

Dur-Katlimmu ■

Apku ■

Tell Moḥammed Arab

Shibaniba ■

Nineveh ■

Kalhu ■

Arbil ■

Kilizu ■

Kar-Tukulti-Ninurta ■

Ashur ■

Arrapha ■

Nuzi ■

Ana

Hit

Dur-Kurigalzu

Sippar

Babylon

Zagros Mts

L Van

L Urmia

Diyala

Tigris

Euphrates

A   B   C

1   2   3

65

ISRAEL AND JUDAH

PHARAOH MERNEPTAH'S VICTORY STELE boasted in 1229 BCE that "Israel is laid waste." He was not referring to a country but to another people who had recently emerged in the Near East.

Below The united kingdom of Israel and Judah: Jerusalem, the capital city, was created by King David and made splendid by his son, King Solomon. When Solomon died the kingdom divided into Israel in the north and Judah in the south.

In 924 BCE the Egyptian pharaoh Shoshenq invaded, but the two kingdoms survived intact until the late 8th century BCE.

THE BIBLE AND ISRAELITE HISTORY

How the Israelites settled in the land of Canaan is recorded in the Bible. The book of Exodus describes their departure from Egypt and the wanderings of the 12 tribes in the Sinai peninsula region. The books of Joshua and Judges tell how the Israelites tried to settle in Canaan. They met with stiff resistance from the local inhabitants and the Philistines who lived on the rich coastal plain.

In about 1080 BCE the Philistines tried to expand their control over the hill country where the Israelite tribes had settled. Faced by this threat, the loosely knit tribes united under the leadership of Saul, the first king of Israel. The two books of Samuel report the development of the Israelite monarchy.

KING DAVID

David was a brilliant king. He was installed as a vassal at Hebron in Judah by the Philistines. Hebron then became the first capital of King David's kingdom. In 995 BCE David threw off the Philistine overlordship and captured Jerusalem, the capital of the Jebusites, a Canaanite tribe.

David made Jerusalem his royal city. It was well placed to control his kingdom, which united Judah in the south with Israel in the north. David also made Jerusalem the religious center of the Israelite nation, bringing there the Ark of the Covenant (the sacred container of the scrolls of Jewish law) that the Philistines had captured earlier.

The Kingdom of Israel and Judah

David, 1000–962 BCE
Reigns 7 years at Hebron, 33 years at Jerusalem, but these periods partly overlap

995 BCE David establishes capital at Jerusalem

Solomon, 962–922 (?) BCE
The date given for Solomon's death varies from 935 to 928 to 922 BCE, depending on the system of calculation used

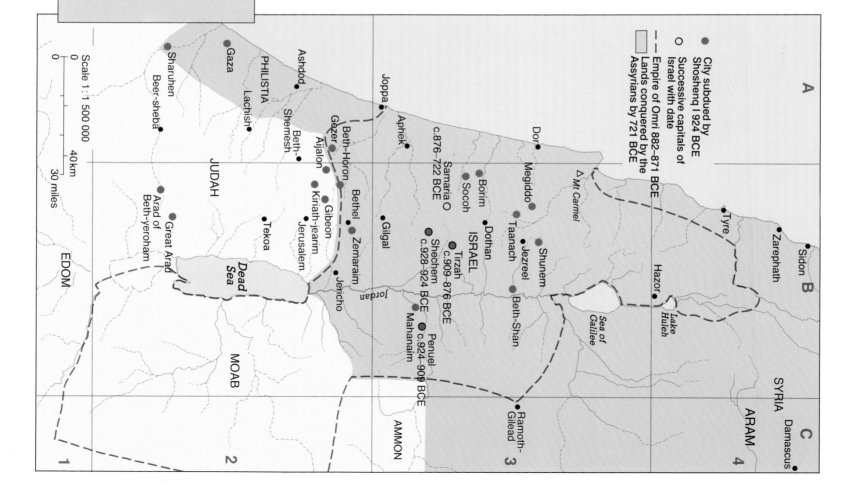

Legend

● City subdued by Shoshenq I 924 BCE

○ Successive capitals of Israel with date

– – Empire of Omri 882–871 BCE

Lands conquered by the Assyrians by 721 BCE

Scale 1:1 500 000

0 — 40km
0 — 30 miles

A Sidon • Damascus **C**
Zarephath •
Tyre •
SYRIA
ARAM

Dor • Mt Carmel
Megiddo
Hazor •
Lake Huleh
Sea of Galilee

Joppa •
Aphek •
Samaria ○ c.876–722 BCE
Borim
Socho
ISRAEL
Dothan
Jezreel
Shunem
Taanach
Beth-Shan
Tirzah ○ c.909–876 BCE
Shechem ● c.928–924 BCE
Mahanaim ● Penuel ○ c.924–909 BCE
Ramoth-Gilead •

Ashdod •
PHILISTIA
Gaza •
Lachish •
Beth-Shemesh •
Gezer •
Beth-Horon •
Aijalon •
Gibeon •
Kiriath-jearim •
Bethel •
Zemaraim •
Jerusalem •
Gilgal •
Jericho •
Jordan
JUDAH
Tekoa •
Dead Sea
Beer-sheba •
Sharuhen •
Arad of Beth-yeroham •
Great Arad •
EDOM
MOAB
AMMON

66

SOLOMON'S ACHIEVEMENTS

King Solomon, David's son, built the Temple in Jerusalem to house the sacred Ark of the Covenant. The Muslim Dome of the Rock now occupies the same site. No trace of Solomon's building has been found, but descriptions are given in the Bible: I Kings, chs 5–8, and 2 Chronicles, chs 2–7. (Herod's temple was built centuries later.)

Solomon also built a palace, using luxury materials, such as ivory and beams of cedar and cypress wood. The design of his palace and the Temple was influenced by styles from Phoenicia, the cosmopolitan northern neighbor of the united kingdom of Israel and Judah.

Outside Jerusalem, there is more archeological evidence of Solomon's building activities. Triple-chambered city gates that he had erected have been found at Megiddo, Hazor, and Gezer. At Megiddo there were also stables for hundreds of horses. Solomon's large army used horse-drawn chariots. At Ezion-Gezer on the Gulf of Aqaba, Solomon had an industrial complex for smelting copper. It was at Ezion-Gezer that Solomon built a fleet of ships to trade on the Red Sea with east Africa and Arabia.

Above The Dome of the Rock is built over the rock where, according to tradition, Abraham was about to sacrifice Isaac, his only son. The beautiful shrine was completed in 691 CE and in medieval times was thought to be the center of the world.

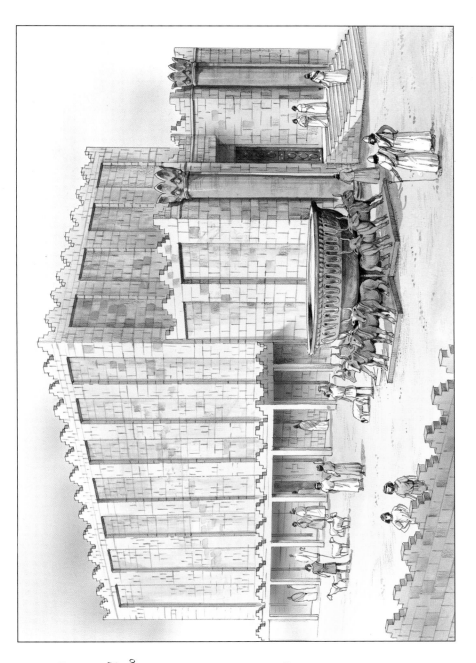

Right Solomon's Temple in Jerusalem. The plan of the building resembled Phoenician architecture. It was rectangular, with a porch flanked by a pair of bronze columns called Jachin and Boaz. The Holy Place was paneled in cedar wood with cypress-wood floors. Only the high priest could enter the Holy of Holies through its double doors. In the temple forecourt a huge bronze basin with water stood supported by 12 bronze bulls. This basin was used for rituals.

MESOPOTAMIAN SITES

KALHU

THE CITY OF KALHU IS IN NORTHERN Iraq, at the join of the Tigris and Great Zab rivers, south of Mosul. The site is also called Nimrud. Kalhu became important when the Assyrian king Ashurnasirpal II (883–859 BCE) selected it as his capital city. Shalmaneser III (858–824 BCE) also built a palace there. Kalhu is mentioned in Genesis, ch. 10, as Calah.

ASHURNASIRPAL'S CITY

By 878 BCE, after Ashurnasirpal II had decided to move his capital from Ashur, a major building program began at Kalhu. A canal was dug from the Great Zab river to provide water. The city was enclosed in massive walls 5mi long that took 70 million bricks to build. Kalhu occupied 900 acres and included a ziggurat, temples, and a magnificent palace.

Ashurnasirpal was very proud of his new capital. An inscription at Kalhu describes a great feast that celebrated the completion of the Northwest Palace. The feasting lasted 10 days, and there were 69,574 guests from all parts of the Assyrian empire.

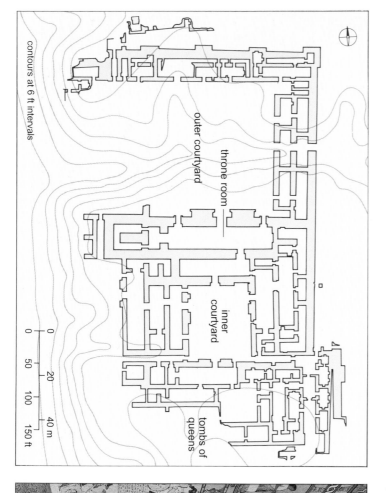

contours at 6 ft intervals

throne room

outer courtyard

inner courtyard

tombs of queens

0 20 40 m
0 50 100 150 ft

Below The Northwest Palace at Kalhu. Around the outer courtyard were offices. The throne room was used for official functions. The king's private quarters were around the inner courtyard.

Above One of the ivory chairbacks that was found in a storage room at Fort Shalmaneser. It was probably made in northern Syria. The Assyrian kings' furniture was often decorated with ivory.

Below How the throne room in the Northwest Palace might have looked — an artist's impression. Colored murals were set above the stone panels, and human-headed lions guarded the entrance.

68

KALHU'S SCULPTURES

Excavations at the city of Kalhu produced some remarkable discoveries. Carved stone panels decorated the courtyard walls and the adjoining throne room of the Northwest Palace. They recorded the king at war and hunting, and fulfilling his religious duties. Ashurnasirpal is also shown receiving gifts, including monkeys, from foreigners. The reliefs, which were once brightly painted, also record in fine detail the fabrics, clothes, and jewelry of the king and his officials.

TREASURES OF KALHU

Kings and courtiers were buried in vaulted chamber tombs. Three royal tombs were excavated at Kalhu, and their treasures were found intact. Gold jewelry was discovered in mint condition.

Thousands of fragments of carved ivory were discovered at an arsenal called Fort Shalmaneser in a well. Many pieces had been war booty collected by the Assyrians during their campaigns in the Levant. They had been hidden there for safe keeping when the Medes sacked Kalhu in 612 BCE.

Right One of the treasures found in the royal tombs at Kalhu. This gold wristlet was set with a precious agate-stone and inlaid with enamel. Gold winged genies hold buckets and pinecones. The wall reliefs at Kalhu show the kings wearing similar wristlets.

Kalhu

LATE ASSYRIAN RULE (1000–750 BCE)

AFTER BEING WEAKENED FOR SEVERAL centuries by the raids of the Aramaeans, the Assyrians grew powerful again in about 900 BCE. Adad-nirari II (911–891 BCE) defeated Babylonia and seized control of the Khabur region in the east. His son Tukulti-Ninurta II (890–884 BCE) and his grandson Ashurnasirpal II (883–859 BCE) continued his military successes.

Ashurnasirpal II went to war every year. Although his claim to be always victorious was probably untrue, in 877 BCE he reached the Mediterranean. He called it "the Great Sea of the land Amurru."

Ashurnasirpal received much tribute from the rich Phoenician states, including "gold, silver, tin, bronze, a bronze cauldron, linen garments with multicolored trimmings, a large female ape and a small female ape, ebony, boxwood, ivory, and sea creatures." He probably used many of these items in the construction of his splendid palace at Kalhu.

Below The Balawat gates, a pair of massive bronze-clad gates built by Shalmaneser III and found 10mi northeast of Kalhu.

The detail here (left) shows chariots with six-spoked wheels, as was the custom in the 9th century, on campaign in Babylonia. Each "leaf" of the gates was about 6.5ft wide and 13ft high. Sixteen embossed bands of bronze were engraved with scenes from Shalmaneser's conquests, including campaigns against the Urartu, who lived in the Lake Van region of present-day Turkey.

SHALMANESER III AND AHAB OF ISRAEL

Shalmaneser III (858–824 BCE) brought Assyrian power to a new height. After conquering the Aramaean state of Bit Adini in 854 BCE, the next year he led his armies against an alliance of kings that included Ben-Hadad of Damascus and Ahab of Israel (869–850 BCE). Ahab had 10,000 foot soldiers and 2,000 chariots.

Shalmaneser was the first Assyrian ruler to come into contact with an Israelite king. After the battle, at Qarqar on the Orontes river, he erected the Black Obelisk (a tall stone monument) at Kalhu and inscribed on it his claims of an overwhelming victory. The biblical account in 1 Kings, ch. 20, suggests that Shalmaneser's success was more limited, but by 838 BCE most states in the region had to pay him tribute.

FRIENDSHIP WITH BABYLON, THEN WAR

In 851 BCE Shalmaneser III helped the king of Babylon defeat a revolt against him. The two kings regarded each other as equals and allies. A throne-base found at Kalhu shows both men clasping hands. Shalmaneser III respected Babylonian religion and visited the temples of Marduk at Babylon and Nabu at Borsippa. He also gave the local citizens gifts and banquets. This was unusual, because the Assyrian king usually demanded vast amounts of tribute.

By the time of Shamshi-Adad V (823–811 BCE), the alliance with Babylon was over, and war broke out between the two kingdoms.

Right Shamsi-Adad V (823–811 BCE) on a stele from Kalhu. The king is in his court robes and is wearing the Assyrian royal headdress and diadem.

Below Detail from the Black Obelisk of Shalmaneser III (858–824 BCE). The cuneiform inscription identifies the man on his knees kissing the ground before the king as the Israelite king Jehu. The camels were tribute from Egypt.

ASSYRIA TRIUMPHANT (750–626 BCE)

Strong kings took the Assyrian empire to the peak of its power between 750 BCE and 626 BCE. They are mentioned in the Bible (2 Kings).

TIGLATH-PILESER III

Tiglath-Pileser III (744–727 BCE) was a successful ruler. He reorganized the army and replaced vassal kings with loyal provincial governors. He introduced a "royal mail" service – his messengers traveled in chariots drawn by mules to all parts of the empire. Tiglath-Pileser III also deported many of the people he conquered to curb future rebellions. Shalmaneser V (726–722 BCE) succeeded his father. Records of his short reign have not survived, but the Bible (2 Kings, ch. 17, verses 3–6) tells how he captured Israel when King Hosea rebelled. Shalmaneser V may have died in the three-year siege of Samaria.

SARGON II

How Sargon (722–705 BCE) came to be king is unknown, but he was a capable leader. At Qarqar, on the Orontes river, Sargon defeated an alliance of Syrian states, establishing Assyrian control as far as Egypt. In Asia Minor he controlled the Phrygians, whose king was the legendary Midas. In 714 BCE he destroyed Musasir, capital of the Urartu. The kings of Cyprus paid tribute to him. In 709 BCE Sargon became king of Babylon, ruling the Near East from The Gulf to the Sinai desert. Sargon was killed in a minor clash in 705 BCE. His body was lost so he could not be buried in his palace.

Below   The Assyrian empire in the late 8th century BCE. The capital city of the empire was Ashur in northern Mesopotamia. The lands controlled by the Assyrians extended from Ur near The Gulf and included the kingdom of Israel. Jerusalem and the kingdom of Judah only came under their control between 733 BCE and 650 BCE. An efficient road system linked the distant parts of the empire, with travelers' rest-houses at regular intervals along the highways.

Kings of Assyria 744–626 BCE

744–727 BCE Tiglath-Pileser III
726–722 BCE Shalmaneser V
722–705 BCE Sargon II
704–681 BCE Sennacherib
680–669 BCE Esarhaddon
668–626 BCE Ashurbanipal

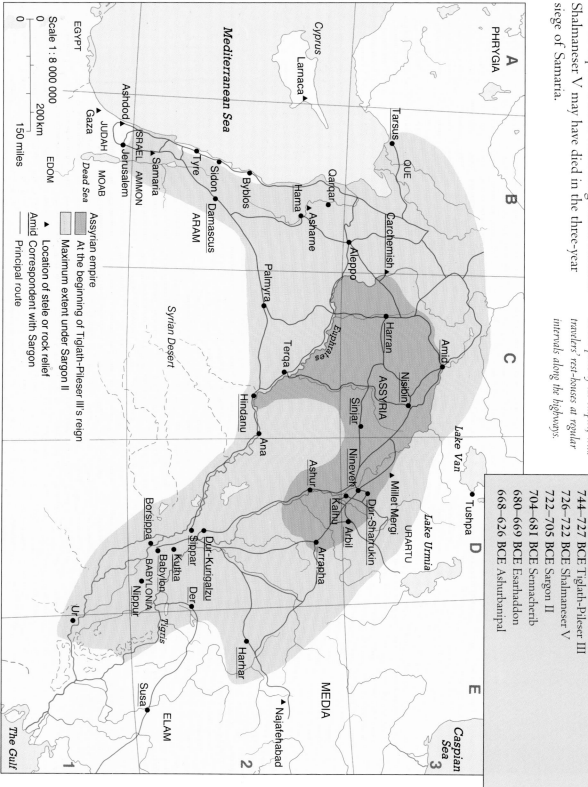

Scale 1:8 000 000

Assyrian empire
At the beginning of Tiglath-Pileser III's reign
Maximum extent under Sargon II

▲ Location of stele or rock relief
Amid Correspondent with Sargon
Principal route

SARGON'S SUCCESSORS

Sennacherib (704–681 BCE) was Sargon's son. His capture of Lachish in 701 BCE and his dealings with Hezekiah, king of Judah, are recorded in the Bible (2 Kings. ch. 18). Problems with Babylon occupied Sennacherib until 694 BCE, when he destroyed the city. One of his own sons then murdered him.

Esarhaddon (680–669 BCE), Sargon's crown prince, then claimed the throne. He captured Memphis from the Egyptians in 671 BCE, but died on a second campaign in 669 BCE.

Esarhaddon's two crown princes succeeded him. Ashurbanipal, king of Assyria, overshadowed his brother, the king of Babylon, both as a military leader and as a man of learning. Ashurbanipal collected many cuneiform texts for his library at Nineveh.

Left A stone carving recording one of the campaigns of the Assyrian kings. Here an Assyrian soldier is shown cutting off the head of the Elamite king whom Ashurbanipal defeated in 635 BCE.

Below A royal procession enters Babylon through the Ishtar gate. It was over 46ft high and made of brilliant blue-glazed bricks decorated with bulls and dragons, symbols of the gods. The king rides in his horse-drawn chariot, sheltered by an umbrella, the symbol of royalty. The first chariot carries his senior court official.

ASHUR

ASHUR LIES ON A ROCKY OUTCROP OF LAND overlooking the Tigris river in northern Iraq. It had been an outpost of southern influence from about 2300 BCE. Sumerian-style statues from the Early Dynastic period and inscriptions were found here.

CITY OF TRADE

Ashur was situated on an important trade route to Anatolia, where in about 2000 BCE merchants from the city established a trading colony at Kanesh. Donkey caravans carried woolen textiles and tin that had been mined in Iran to Ashur, from where they were distributed farther afield. Many cuneiform tablets discovered at Kanesh show that a lively correspondence went on between the two depots.

ASSYRIAN CAPITAL

Although Ashur was well placed for trade, it was not an obvious site for the capital of a kingdom, because of the lack of farmland around it. Despite this, the Middle and Late Assyrian rulers favored the city.

Adad-nirari I (1305–1274 BCE) built a large palace at Ashur. Tukulti-Ninurta I (1243–1207 BCE) dug a moat around the western side of the city, which was open to attack. He also rebuilt the Ishtar temple and started work on a new palace. Ashur kept its reputation as a religious center even after Ashurnasirpal II (883–859 BCE) shifted his capital to Kalhu. There was a ziggurat and many temples, apart from the major shrine to Ashur, the city god who was a combination of the Sumerian god Enlil and the Babylonian deity Marduk. The tombs of five Assyrian kings have been found at Ashur. These include those of Ashurnasirpal II and Shamsi-Adad V (823–811 BCE), who built or reconstructed most of the public and religious buildings. Later Assyrian kings built three ziggurats and at least 38 temples inside the 346-acre city.

Between 614 BCE and 612 BCE the Medes from Iran invaded Assyria and looted Ashur. In the 1st and 2nd centuries it was resettled and became known as Labbana. Now the site is threatened by flooding from a proposed dam farther upstream on the Tigris.

Above The tomb and sarcophagus (stone coffin) of the Middle Assyrian king Ashur-belkals (1074–1057 BCE), one of five royal burial places discovered at Ashur.

Below The site of Ashur. There were many temples, including the temple of the city god, also called Ashur. The palace, the ziggurat and the temples were sited on the steep northern cliffs overlooking the old course of the Tigris. The river now flows on the eastern side of the promontory. The western side was protected by a wall and a moat.

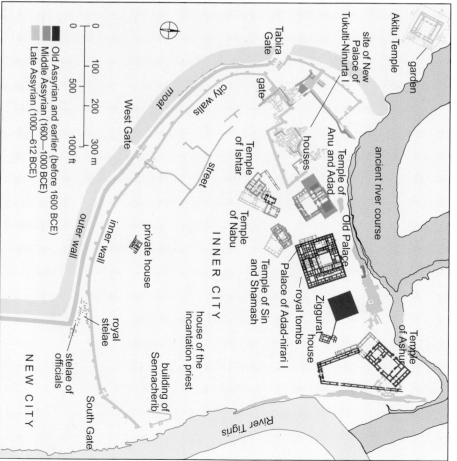

Akitu Temple

garden

site of New Palace of
Tukulti-Ninurta I

Tabira Gate

gate

houses

Temple of Ishtar

Temple of Anu and Adad

Temple of Old Palace

ancient river course

Temple of Nabu

Temple of Sin and Shamash

Palace of Adad-nirari I

royal tombs

Ziggurat

house

Temple of Ashur

private house

house of the incantation priest

INNER CITY

building of Sennacherib

royal stelae

stelae of officials

West Gate

moat

city walls

street

outer wall

inner wall

NEW CITY

South Gate

River Tigris

0 — 100 — 200 — 300 m
0 — 500 — 1000 ft

Old Assyrian and earlier (before 1600 BCE)
Middle Assyrian (1600—1000 BCE)
Late Assyrian (1000—612 BCE)

NINEVEH

NINEVEH WAS ONE OF THE GREATEST CITIES of Mesopotamia. It is situated on the eastern side of the Tigris river near modern Mosul in northern Iraq. It stood on one of the major western trade routes to the Mediterranean. The site was enclosed by more than 7½mi of city walls and has two main mounds: Nebi Yunus (the citadel) and Kuyunjik (the arsenal).

Under the dynasty of Agade, Manishtushu (2269–2255 BCE) founded the famous temple of Ishtar at Nineveh, mentioned by Hammurabi in his law code. Here was found the superb bronze life-sized head of Naram-Sin (2254–2218 BCE), one of the great Mesopotamian art treasures.

The Late Assyrian ruler Sennacherib (705–681 BCE) made Nineveh his capital. His Southwest Palace was decorated with carved stone reliefs showing, among other scenes, the siege and capture of Lachish. Sennacherib's grandson Ashurbanipal (669–627 BCE) built the North Palace on Kuyunjik, for his cuneiform library.

Genesis, ch. 10, verse 11, mentions Nineveh, and the biblical books of Nahum and Jonah prophesy the city's downfall. In 612 BCE Nineveh was destroyed by the Babylonians and Medes. Its fall marked the collapse of the Assyrian empire.

Right A reconstruction of the walls and towers at Nineveh. The mound of Nebi Yunus (the citadel) is the traditional Muslim burial site of the prophet Jonah.

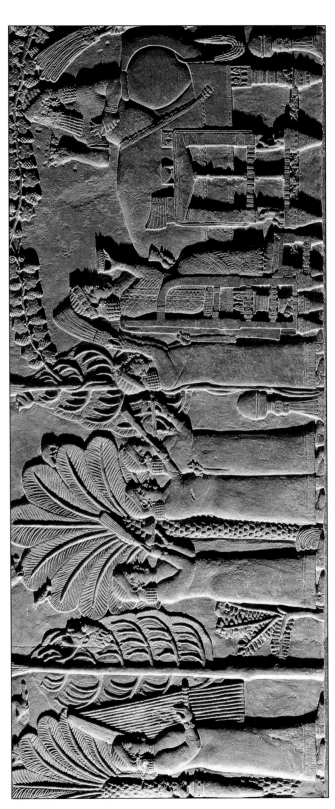

Below Ashurbanipal and his queen Ashur-sharrat feast in their gardens – possibly those of the Northwest Palace at Nineveh, where the carving was found. In the pine tree on the left hangs the head of an enemy king.

WARFARE

THE FIRST WEAPONS WERE THE STONE AND wooden tools used to hunt animals: arrowheads, clubs, spears, and slings. Then came metal weapons. Copper axes, spears, and daggers were in use by about 4000 BCE. There were bronze weapons by about 2000 BCE, and iron 1,000 years later.

HOW EARLY WARS WERE FOUGHT

Armies were well organized. The Sumerian "Stele of the Vultures," dated 2450 BCE, shows soldiers from Lagash. The men march in military formation with their spears and axes, protected by their shields, behind their leader, Eannatum. In Sumer, the warrior-lugals or "great men" became the first kings.

The first fortified city was Jericho, whose massive walls (they still stand 13ft high) and a round tower 26ft high were built as long ago as 9000 BCE. As more cities constructed similar defenses, siege warfare developed as a way of capturing these places. Military machinery, such as battering rams and siege towers, came into use by about 1000 BCE.

Horses revolutionized war. Slow-moving carts drawn by mules had been used in Sumerian times. In about 1500 BCE the first two-wheeled horse-drawn war-chariots were used. Cavalry units, introduced by the Assyrians, rode bareback, because the saddle had not yet been invented.

Left Assyrian cavalrymen from the reliefs at the Northwest Palace at Kalhu. The men ride in pairs, one steering the horses, and the other shooting with bow and arrow. Their defeated enemies lie trampled and decapitated under the horses' hooves.

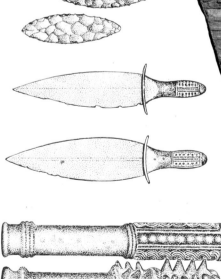

Above Flints (left) were still used for arrowheads after metal weapons were cast. Personal weapons, such as these daggers (middle), were often beautifully decorated. Maces (right) were both weapons and symbols of royal authority — just the heads are shown here.

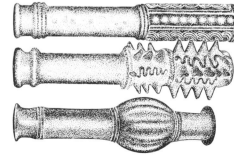

Left The "Stele of the Vultures" is the first known carving showing an army at war. On the lower part of this fragment, King Eannatum rides in a chariot, followed by his foot soldiers. This may be a victory parade to celebrate the success of the war shown in the upper part of the fragment.

THE ASSYRIAN ARMY

The Assyrian army was a well-developed fighting machine, with as many as 50,000 troops. It received its supplies through taxes, tribute, and war booty. Some of the soldiers were mercenaries – foreign professional soldiers who fought for money.

The king was always the commander-in-chief of the army. Provincial governors often acted as the generals. Sometimes senior palace officials also led the troops. Tiglath-Pileser III (744–727 BCE) appointed his chief eunuch commander of his chariot forces. Before going into battle, kings would consult omen-tellers who would reveal the will of the gods.

THE INFANTRY

The infantry or foot soldiers were a large and important part of the Assyrian army. The men came from the poorer families or were slaves sent by their wealthy owners.

The light infantry uniform was a short tunic, a cone-shaped helmet and a lightweight shield made of wicker and leather. The heavy infantry uniform was a long robe covered with metal plates. This was one of the earliest forms of chain mail and made a weighty load. The weapons of the infantryman included a sling (for throwing stones), a longbow, and a pike.

It was the job of the infantry to force its way through holes broken in the walls of cities being besieged. Archers were positioned in the top of assault towers which were made of wicker and leather on a wooden frame. The towers were wheeled and had battering rams.

CHARIOT WARFARE

Fewer in number than the infantry, the chariot troops of the Assyrian army were usually highborn Assyrians. They were the army's elite. Chariots were manned by a charioteer and an archer, sometimes protected by two shield-bearers. Chariots were drawn by two horses, sometimes with a third horse not yoked to the chariot but kept as a spare to replace an exhausted beast in battle. A tablet from Amarna includes the words "I have sent . . . precious stones, 15 pairs of horses for five wooden chariots."

The body of the chariots was square and probably made of wickerwork, with the wheel axle at the back end. Chariots were open at the back. Spears, the battle ax, and other weapons were kept in a box attached to the front.

Right A crescent-shaped bronze axhead dating from about 2400 BCE. The axhead was fitted into a slot in the haft (wooden handle) and fastened with nails or bolts. Other axheads were cast in metal with a hole to take the haft.

Below The art of war in Assyrian times. The bronze panels of the Balawat gates show scenes from the wars fought by the Assyrians. Here an Assyrian siege engine, with archers on top, attacks a city in northern Syria. Siege warfare was an important part of the Assyrians' method of conquest and is depicted in their reliefs.

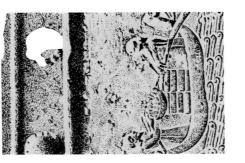

Below This detail from the Balawat gates shows Phoenician boats bringing tribute from the island of Tyre to the mainland for Shalmaneser III. Both the Assyrians and, later, the Persians used the famous Phoenician navy in warfare.

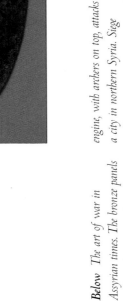

Left An Assyrian war-chariot, from the Balawat gates. Shalmaneser III's chariot forces were the very best part of his army. Chariots were also used for hunting and in ceremonial processions. In the late 8th century BCE cavalry became more important, especially for fighting in the mountains, where chariots could not go.

T HE LATE ASSYRIAN PERIOD WAS A troubled time for Babylon, which had 24 kings between 900 BCE and 681 BCE. The city's fortunes changed when Esarhaddon (680–669 BCE) became king. By the end of the next century Babylon became rich, powerful, and famous.

NABOPOLASSAR

Nabopolassar (625–605 BCE), who claimed to be the "son of a nobody," founded the New Babylonian dynasty. After 10 years of fighting the Assyrians in the Babylonian territories, Nabopolassar gained enough power to march north. He intended to attack Ashur, the religious capital of the Assyrians.

Before Nabopolassar could strike, Ashur was overrun by the Medes, from northwest Iran. The Babylonian and Median armies joined forces and in 612 BCE captured Nineveh, looting the palaces and temples.

In 1990 a tangled mass of skeletons was excavated at one of the city's gates – evidence of Nineveh's population trying to flee.

Neo-Babylonian kings
The Chaldean dynasty, 625–562 BCE

625–605 BCE	Nabopolassar
614 BCE	Destruction of Ashur
612 BCE	Sack of Nineveh
605–562 BCE	Nebuchadrezzar
605 BCE	Defeat of Pharaoh Necho at Carchemish, in Syria

Kings of Judah, 640–587 BCE

640–609 BCE	Josiah Josiah takes advantage of Assyria's weakness to re-establish the Davidic kingdom but is killed in 609 BCE by Pharaoh Necho II at Megiddo
609–598 BCE	Jehoiakim
598–597 BCE	Jehoiachin
597 BCE	Jehoiachin deported to Babylon
597–587 BCE	Zedekiah
587 BCE	Siege of Jerusalem, destruction of the Temple, deportation of citizens to Babylon

Below Nebuchadrezzar and his wife relax in the beautiful Hanging Gardens of Babylon. They are being fanned by servants and entertained by a court musician playing a harp. The king and queen wear embroidered garments decorated with sequins made of gold. They are enjoying drinks chilled with ice from the royal icehouse. An icehouse of Zimri-Lim at Mari dating from about 2000 BCE.

Above This black stone tablet has an inscription recording the rebuilding of Babylon and its temples by Esarhaddon (the city's king from 680 BCE to 669 BCE). It shows the Assyrian king holding his mace, the symbol of royal power, and standing respectfully before a temple. Just behind him is the sacred tree of life and the bull, symbol of the weather god. The plow below suggests the agricultural and economic wealth that Esarhaddon restored to Babylon.

Zedekiah also rebelled. The Babylonians laid siege to Jerusalem, and broke through its defenses in 587–586 BCE. They destroyed much of the city, deporting the Jewish population (many to Babylon) and carrying away treasures from the Temple. The Bible records these events in the books of 2 Kings, 2 Chronicles and Jeremiah.

NEBUCHADREZZAR'S GREAT CITY

We know quite a lot about the outline of the city from a cuneiform text but it was Nebuchadrezzar who was responsible for rebuilding the city and restoring Babylon's wealth and reputation. He took a leading role in the great Akitu festival, marking the Babylonian New Year. He carried out massive rebuilding programs at the temple of Marduk and the ziggurat, as well as constructing the fabled Hanging Gardens for one of his wives, who was homesick for the mountains of her native Media. Nebuchadrezzar also surrounded Babylon with walls that encircled an area of more than 3 sq mi.

Above A reconstruction of the Ishtar gate in the Museum of the Ancient Orient in Berlin. The gate originally stood between the outer and inner walls of the city of Babylon. The processional way ran from it to the sacred area of the city. The great processions that took place during the 11-day Akitu or New Year festival would have passed through the gate.

The bulls and dragons on the gate are made from molded baked bricks. Bulls were the symbol of Adad, god of thunder. Dragons were the symbols of Marduk, the city god of Babylon.

NEBUCHADREZZAR

Before he became king, Nebuchadrezzar, Nabopolassar's son and crown-prince, had tasted success in battle. In 605 BCE he defeated the Egyptian pharaoh Necho at Carchemish in northern Syria. He left the kingdom of Judah alone, because King Jehoiakim had paid him tribute. On the death of his father in 605 BCE, Nebuchadrezzar returned to Babylon to be crowned king. He had marched for three weeks, covering over 30 mi a day, to return for his coronation.

BABYLON AND THE JEWS

Jehoiakim (609–598 BCE) succeeded his father Josiah (640–609 BCE) as king of Judah. He accepted Nebuchadrezzar as his overlord. Then, in 601–600 BCE, Jehoiakim rebelled. Nebuchadrezzar captured Jerusalem in 597 BCE. He took Judah's new king, Jehoiachin, the son of Jehoiakim, and his mother, wives, and officials in chains to Babylon. Nebuchadrezzar appointed Jehoiachin's uncle, Zedekiah (597–587 BCE), king of Judah. But

BABYLON

"**B**ABYLON SURPASSES IN SPLENDOR ANY city of the known world," wrote the Greek historian Herodotus, who visited Babylon in about 450 BCE. The site is about 50mi south of Baghdad, in present-day Iraq. The city became important under Hammurabi (1792–1750 BCE). But it resisted Assyrian rule and was destroyed by Sennacherib (705–681 BCE).

In the Neo-Babylonian period, Babylon was capital of the empire. Nebopolassar and his son Nebuchadrezzar (605–562 BCE) carried out a huge building program. The city remained important under the later Persian rulers, opening its gates to Cyrus in 539 BCE. The Persian kings then made Babylon their winter residence. Alexander the Great also entered the city without resistance. When Alexander's general Seleucus built his new capital farther along the Tigris river, Babylon sank into decline.

"GATES OF THE GODS"

The name Babylon means "gate of the gods." The site was roughly rectangular and had a double wall of defense. The main route across the city was the processional way. Entry to the city was through eight gateways, each protected by a god or goddess. The most spectacular was the gate dedicated to Ishtar, with its brilliant blue tiles decorated with bulls and dragons.

THE HANGING GARDENS

Ancient historians rated the Hanging Gardens of Babylon as one of the Seven Wonders of the World. Nebuchadrezzar built them for his wife Amityia. The Hanging Gardens must have seemed marvelous to the travelers who came to this otherwise hot and dusty city. The site of the famous gardens has not been found, nor that of the Tower of Babel which is mentioned in the Bible.

Below Ancient Babylon covered an area of over 2,150 acres – larger than many modern towns. At the time of Nebuchadrezzar, the Euphrates river flowed through the city, dividing it into two sections, which were connected by a bridge. In the older, eastern part (left) was the king's palace, near the Ishtar gate (bottom left). From here the processional way led toward the great temple of Marduk and the ziggurat (top center). The western part of Babylon (right) was probably a residential area.

Left A glazed relief brick panel from Darius' palace at Susa. The winged lion has ram's horns and is decorated in blues and greens. Embossed colored tiles developed because of the lack of stone in the region.

Above Basalt statue of the lion of Babylon trampling a man beneath him. This was found in the ruins of the Northern Palace, which was built by Nebuchadrezzar. It was part of a "museum" belonging to the king.

THE PERSIAN EMPIRE (560–521 BCE)

CYRUS BECAME KING OF THE PERSIANS IN 559 BCE. The Median king Astyges was his overlord. Other rulers of the time were Croesus of Lydia and Nabonidus of Babylon. Cyrus conquered all three kings and founded the Persian empire, which dominated the Near East for the next 200 years.

THE CONQUESTS OF CYRUS

Cyrus was king between 559 BCE and 530 BCE. In 550 BCE he turned against Astyges, king of the Medes. The Medes had overrun the cities of Ashur, Kalhu, and Nineveh in 612–614 BCE, ending the Assyrian dynasty. Now Cyrus marched to the Median capital at Hamadan, emptied the treasury and took possession of vast lands from Turkey to Central Asia.

In 547 BCE Cyrus led his armies to the western borders of his empire to do battle with the Lydians. Croesus, the Lydian king, was legendary for his wealth. There was gold in his lands, and the Lydians may have been the first people to use large numbers of coins, stamped to guarantee their quality and weight. Croesus' territories included the Greek cities of

the Aegean coast. When Croesus heard of Cyrus' defeat of the Medes, he thought he could expand his empire. He consulted the oracle at Delphi before going to war and learned that a great empire would be destroyed. Croesus did not realize that the empire to be destroyed was his — at the hands of Cyrus.

BABYLON: JEWEL IN CYRUS' CROWN

The Babylonian king Nabonidus (555–539 BCE) was more than 60 years old when he came to the throne. He rebuilt the temple to Sin in Harran and installed his daughter as the priestess of Sin at Ur. This was a time of poverty, plague, and famine in Babylon. For unknown reasons, Nabonidus left Babylon to live in Taima, in northwest Arabia. He left his son Belshazzar to rule in his place, and for 10 years the Akitu or New Year's festival could not be celebrated, because there was no king.

Nabonidus was unpopular with the people of Babylon for neglecting the religion of the city's god, Marduk. In 539 BCE the Akitu festival was celebrated, as is described by the Greek historians and the biblical book of Daniel. The end of the Babylonian dynasty had arrived.

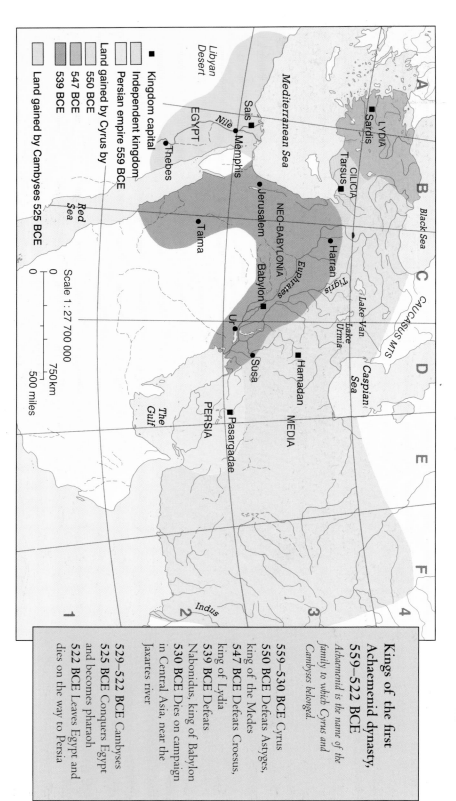

Below The growth of the Persian empire. Cyrus' vast lands stretched from the coast of the Mediterranean to the Indus valley. The Persians had been ruled by the Medes when Cyrus became king. Within a few years he had conquered the territories of the Medes, which stretched to Central Asia in the east, the Babylonian lands in the south, and the Lydian kingdom, in modern Turkey, in the west. Cyrus' son Cambyses also controlled Egypt.

Map legend

- Kingdom capital
- Independent kingdom
- Persian empire 559 BCE
- Land gained by Cyrus by 559 BCE
- 550 BCE
- 547 BCE
- 539 BCE
- Land gained by Cambyses 525 BCE

Scale 1 : 27 700 000

0 ___ 500 miles
0 ___ 750km

Labels: Libyan Desert, Mediterranean Sea, Black Sea, Sais, Memphis, EGYPT, Nile, Thebes, Red Sea, LYDIA, Sardis, Tarsus, CILICIA, Jerusalem, Harran, NEO-BABYLONIA, Babylon, Euphrates, Tigris, Taima, Ur, The Gulf, Susa, Hamadan, MEDIA, PERSIA, Pasargadae, Lake Van, Lake Urmia, Caspian Sea, CAUCASUS MTS, Indus

Grid: A B C D E F / 1 2 3 4

Kings of the first Achaemenid dynasty, 559–522 BCE

Achaemenid is the name of the family to which Cyrus and Cambyses belonged.

559–530 BCE Cyrus
550 BCE Defeats Astyges, king of the Medes
547 BCE Defeats Croesus, king of Lydia
539 BCE Defeats Nabonidus, king of Babylon
530 BCE Dies on campaign in Central Asia, near the Jaxartes river

529–522 BCE Cambyses
525 BCE Conquers Egypt and becomes pharaoh
522 BCE Leaves Egypt and dies on the way to Persia

Cyrus arrived with his army at Babylon in 539 BCE and entered the city without a battle. The Babylonians did not resist. Many of them, celebrating a religious festival, did not even know. Cyrus told his troops not to damage the city or its temples.

FOUNDATION OF THE PERSIAN EMPIRE

Cyrus proclaimed himself "king of the world, great king . . . king of Babylon, king of Sumer and Akkad." The Greek historians considered him a model ruler. He allowed the Jews who had been exiled in Babylon by Nebuchadrezzar to return to Jerusalem and rebuild the Temple, as the biblical book of Ezra relates.

Cyrus used Lydian craftsmen to build his capital at Pasargadae, in modern Iran. He was buried there in 530 BCE after being killed in battle in Central Asia.

Cyrus' son, Cambyses (529–522 BCE), expanded the empire to include Egypt, which he conquered in 525 BCE. Cambyses had the reputation of being a tyrant. He lived in Egypt and acted like a pharaoh. In 522 BCE he left Egypt to return to Persia but died on the way.

Above Cyrus had his own tomb built at Pasargadae, his capital. It is a simple gabled building set on a stepped platform. Cyrus' modesty is shown in an inscription that was on the tomb: "I am Cyrus, who founded the empire of the Persians and was king of Asia. Grudge me not therefore this monument."

Right Remains of a palace at Pasargadae. The city's palaces were inspired by Median architecture and are not like those in Mesopotamia. They had columned halls and open porticoes which allowed access to the beautiful gardens in which they were set. Lydian stonemasons may have made the columns, which are similar to ones found at Ephesus in western Turkey.

DARIUS' EMPIRE (521–486 BCE)

DARIUS (521–486 BCE) RULED THE Persian empire after Cambyses. Under his brilliant rule, the empire reached into Europe, but he had come to the throne only after a struggle.

THE BEHISTUN INSCRIPTION

Darius told the world about his fight to become king, after Cambyses died in 522 BCE, in the famous inscription of Behistun. Carved on a rock overlooking the main caravan route from Babylon to Hamadan in northern Iran, the inscription is in three languages: Old Persian, Babylonian, and Elamite.

Darius claimed that after Cambyses murdered his own brother, Bardiya, before setting out to Egypt, a priest called Gaumata seized the throne. He pretended to be Bardiya and was accepted as king. Nobody dared resist Gaumata until Darius killed him in 522 BCE.

The real truth is probably that Darius took the Persian throne by force from Cambyses' brother. Darius did belong to the Achaemenid family, after which the dynasty is named, but was not in direct line to the throne.

Rebellions broke out in many parts of the Persian empire after Cambyses died. Within a year Darius had established his rule over the kings of Persia, Elam, Media, Assyria, Egypt, Parthia, Margian, Sattagydia, and Scythia. This achievement is recorded on the relief accompanying the Behistun inscription. The carving shows Darius

Below Building materials for the palace at Susa. Darius made Susa the capital of his huge empire. He imported materials from every corner of his territories to build his palace there. In 500 BCE he built a canal from the river Nile to the Red Sea, making it much easier to bring goods by ship from Egypt. Darius was proud of the resources used and left inscriptions at Susa listing the people and materials involved in building his palace.

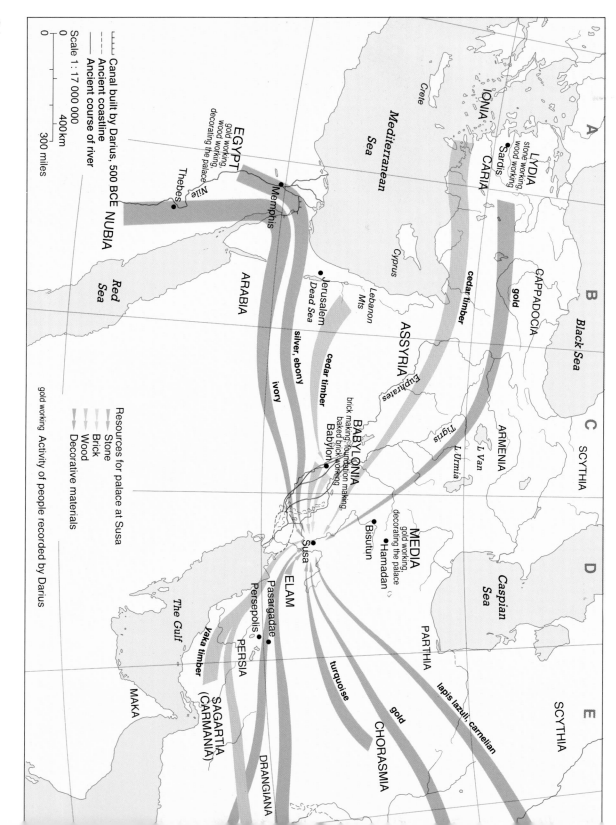

Canal built by Darius, 500 BCE
Ancient coastline
Ancient course of river

Scale 1:17 000 000
0   400km
0   300 miles

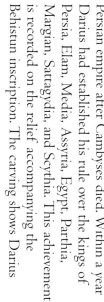

Resources for palace at Susa
Stone
Brick
Wood
Decorative materials

gold working — Activity of people recorded by Darius

EGYPT
gold working,
wood working,
decorating the palace
Thebes
Nile
Memphis
NUBIA
Red Sea
ARABIA

Mediterranean Sea
Crete
IONIA
CARIA
Sardis
LYDIA
stone working,
wood working
gold
CAPPADOCIA
Black Sea
SCYTHIA

Cyprus
Lebanon Mts
Jerusalem
Dead Sea
cedar timber
silver, ebony
cedar timber
ivory
ASSYRIA
Euphrates
Tigris
ARMENIA
L. Van
L. Urmia
MEDIA
gold working,
decorating the palace
Bisutun
Hamadan
Caspian Sea
PARTHIA
lapis lazuli, carnelian
SCYTHIA

BABYLONIA
brick making, foundation making,
baked brick working
Babylon
Susa
ELAM
Pasargadae
Persepolis
PERSIA
SAGARTIA
(CARMANIA)
Yaka timber
turquoise
gold
CHORASMIA
DRANGIANA

The Gulf
MAKA

THE PERSIAN EMPIRE UNDER DARIUS

Darius' empire reached from Central Asia to Egypt. He ruled by dividing it into 20 provinces and appointing a governor to each. He conquered the Indus region and in 513 BCE campaigned against the Scythians in Thrace, on the Black Sea. He went into Europe, crossing the river Danube.

In 499 BCE the Greeks who lived in Cyprus and on the Aegean coast of Turkey rebelled against the Persians. The Ionian revolt lasted six years. Darius used the Phoenician navy to regain Cyprus, but the Greek cities on the Turkish coast were harder to control.

In 494 BCE a naval battle took place off the island of Lade, near Miletus. The Persian fleet of 600 ships overwhelmed the much smaller Greek navy. Darius now turned his attention to mainland Greece, but the Greeks defeated the Persian army at Marathon in 490 BCE.

Darius died in 486 BCE. His son Xerxes inherited a very well-organized empire, with a regular taxation system and efficient communications. Like the Assyrians before them, the Persians relied on a quick horseback messenger service with relay stations providing fresh mounts.

under the winged standard of Ahura-Mazda, the great god of the Zoroastrian religion, receiving the homage of the nine kings.

Darius believed that he had been chosen to rule by the supreme god, Ahura-Mazda. He thought that kingship was a gift from the gods and that kings had special responsibilities to their people.

At Naqsh-i Rastam, where Darius was buried in a rock-cut tomb, an inscription proclaimed that Darius had been made king by Ahura-Mazda; he was a friend to good and an enemy to evil; he protected the weak from the strong and also the strong from the weak; he desired what was right; he was a good horseman, a good archer, and a good spearman.

Above Darius was king over many nations. Delegations brought gifts to him, as shown in this stone carving. The Bactrian (from Bactria in Central Asia) holds a pair of bracelets similar to some found in Afghanistan today.

Below This molded and glazed brick panel from Susa was made in the 12th century BCE but was thrown away by Darius. This form of ornamental brickwork was first produced by the Kassites in Mesopotamia then used by the Persians.

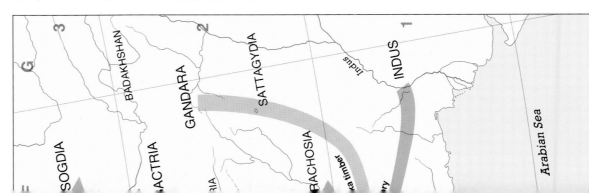

SOGDIA

BADAKHSHAN

BACTRIA

GANDARA

RIA

SATTAGYDIA

RACHOSIA

Indus

INDUS

Arabian Sea

G 3

2

1

SITES

SUSA

USA IS SITUATED ON THE PLAINS OF Khuzestan in southwest Iran. In about 2500 BCE the city was the capital of Elam, which had links with the Fars region and with Anshan to the southeast. With the rise of the dynasty of Agade in 2300 BCE Susa came under Mesopotamian control. In 2004 BCE it was reunited with Anshan, beginning the Elamite era. Almost 800 years later, in one of the most brilliant periods of their history, the Elamites overran Mesopotamia and brought its finest art treasures as war booty to Susa.

Ashurbanipal (668–627 BCE) captured Susa and completely destroyed it. He sowed the fields with salt so that no crops could grow.

Left A glazed brick relief from Darius' palace at Susa. The archer was probably a member of Darius' bodyguard. This decorated brickwork may have been made by Mesopotamian workers who were brought to Susa.

Below The fronts of two bulls placed together made the column capitals (topmost parts) for the palace at Susa. A heavy wooden beam rested on the animals' backs.

CITY OF DARIUS

The time of the Persian empire was a golden period for Susa. The city blossomed under Darius the Great (522–486 BCE), who made it his administrative capital. On the Apadana mound of the city he built a large palace, using workers and luxury materials from all parts of the Persian empire, and combining Babylonian and Median architecture.

Darius' palace at Susa is mentioned in the biblical books of Esther and Nehemiah, where the city is called Shushan.

Alexander the Great captured Susa in 331 BCE. To cement his empire together, he arranged the mass marriage of Greek soldiers and Persian women there. The tomb of the biblical prophet Daniel is thought to be near the acropolis area, now the village of Shush, and is still visited by Muslim pilgrims.

Left This gold statue of a man with a kid is one of a pair. The other is made from silver. Both statues were probably gifts of thanks made by a private person to the temple at Susa. They are not Persian but from an earlier period, about 1100 BCE.

Below The site of Susa, which was identified in 1851, has four mounds. Three of these – the palace, the acropolis or "high place," which was the main religious center, and the royal city – belong to the period of the Persian empire.

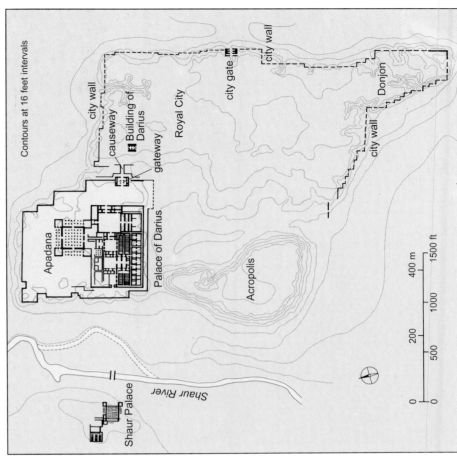

87

THE FINAL YEARS (486–323 BCE)

THE LAST YEARS OF THE PERSIAN EMPIRE were a time of struggle with the Greeks. The Persians gained some early victories, but these were followed by defeats.

XERXES AGAINST THE GREEKS

Darius' son Xerxes (486–465 BCE) was his chosen successor. According to Herodotus, the Greek historian, Xerxes led 2 million men against Greece in 480 BCE. He captured Athens, but the Greek navy defeated the Persian fleet at the battle of Salamis. Xerxes returned to Persia, leaving his general Mardonius in command. After an undecided land battle at Plataia in 479 BCE, the Persian armies left Greece, but the Persian fleet was again defeated, this time at Mycale in Ionia.

MURDER IN THE PERSIAN COURT

Despite the Greek defeats, the Persian empire remained intact until Xerxes died, or was perhaps killed by three of his courtiers, in 465 BCE. Now the Persian court entered a period of plots and multiple murders, often by poisoning. One of Xerxes' sons killed another. Then, in 425 BCE, three of Xerxes' grandsons ruled in quick succession, the first two being murdered after only a few months on the throne. More royal conspiracies and murders followed for almost 100 years.

DARIUS III AND ALEXANDER

Darius III (335–330 BCE) had managed to survive all the palace plots. But in 334 BCE a greater problem arose. Alexander of Macedon, known as Alexander the Great, led his army against the Persian empire. Alexander's troops defeated Darius' time after time, and in 331 BCE, near Babylon, Darius fled the battlefield, only to be killed by his courtiers.

Alexander took command of the entire Persian empire. He now ruled the great cities of Babylon, Susa, Persepolis, and Hamadan. The empire of Cyrus and Darius which had survived for 150 years was at an end, and so was the great civilization of the ancient Near East.

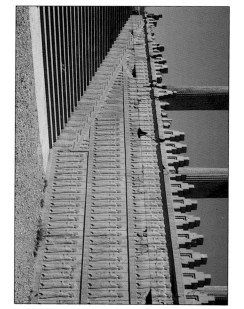

Left A procession of the soldiers of all nations lines the stairway at Persepolis leading into the Apadana palace. Darius I began to build the city of Persepolis. His son Xerxes continued the work and his grandson Artaxerxes completed it.

Right The empire of Alexander the Great. When Alexander defeated Darius III at Gaugamela in 331 BCE, he became lord of all the Persian territories, which extended to Central Asia and India. When he died at the age of 33, his generals divided up the vast kingdom between them. The Near East went to Seleucus, and Egypt was governed by Ptolemy.

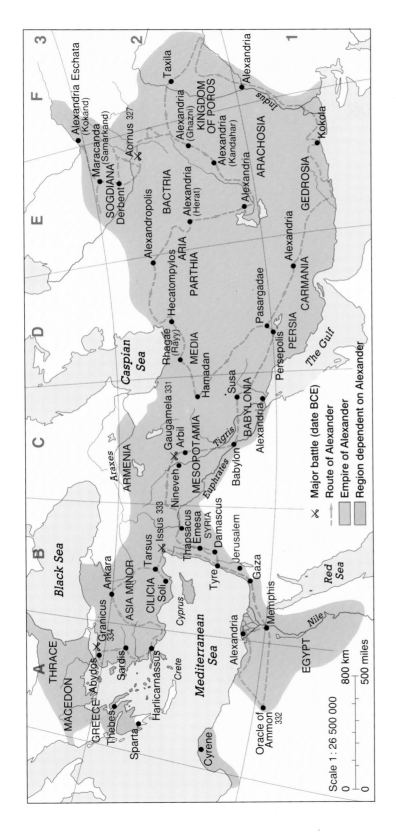

Scale 1 : 26 500 000

0   800 km
0   500 miles

✕ Major battle (date BCE)
→ Route of Alexander
   Empire of Alexander
   Region dependent on Alexander

Map labels:

THRACE
MACEDON
GREECE
Thebes
Sparta
Abydos ✕ Granicus 334
Ankara
Sardis
ASIA MINOR
Halicarnassus
Crete
Tarsus
CILICIA
Soli
Cyprus
Issus 333 ✕
Thapsacus
Emesa
Damascus
SYRIA
Tyre
Jerusalem
Gaza
Memphis
Alexandria
EGYPT
Nile
Oracle of Ammon 332
Cyrene
Red Sea
Mediterranean Sea
Black Sea

ARMENIA
Araxes
Nineveh ✕ Gaugamela 331
Arbil
MESOPOTAMIA
Tigris
Euphrates
Babylon
BABYLONIA
Alexandria
Susa
Hamadan
MEDIA
Rhagae (Rayy)
Hecatompylos
PARTHIA
ARIA
Alexandropolis
Caspian Sea

Pasargadae
Persepolis
PERSIA
Alexandria
CARMANIA
The Gulf

Derbent
SOGDIANA
Maracanda (Samarkand)
Alexandria Eschata (Kokand)
Aornus 327 ✕
BACTRIA
Alexandria (Ghazni)
Alexandria (Herat)
Alexandria (Kandahar)
ARACHOSIA
GEDROSIA
Alexandria

Taxila
KINGDOM OF POROS
Alexandria
Indus
Kokola

F   E   D   C   B   A

3   2   1

Right The main reception hall of the Apadana palace at Persepolis. Here the king would receive important foreign visitors. The columns are almost 66ft high and have ornate capitals in the shape of bulls or lions. Columned halls were typical of Persian architecture.

Left Alexander the Great (356–323 BCE) leads his armies on a campaign. His conquests stretched from his native Macedonia and Greece to the Indus river in Asia. In battle against the Indian king Porbates, Alexander crossed the Indus. His army defeated the Indians, whose elephants panicked in battle. But Alexander's Greek troops were homesick, so he decided to begin the long march back to Greece. Reaching Babylon in 323 BCE, Alexander, the invincible warrior, caught a fever and soon died.

WAR AND LOOTING

BOOTY WAS PART OF WAR IN THE ANCIENT Near East. In 1159 BCE the Elamites sacked Babylon, taking the sacred treasures of the Mesopotamians. The stele of Naram-Sin, Hammurabi's law code, and statues of Nanna from Uruk and Marduk from Babylon were all seized. Some of these priceless treasures were never returned and were discovered, by chance, at Susa last century. Antiquities (objects from ancient times) command high prices. In 1880 three merchants were robbed in Afghanistan of their gold treasure, named after the river where it was discovered, was given to the British Museum.

Gold objects are highly sought after, because they are easily sold or simply melted down into bars. The gold treasure from the royal tombs at Kalhu was put in a bank vault in Baghdad during the 1991 Gulf War, but its fate remains unknown. Trade in stolen or illegal goods is profitable and still, unfortunately, on the increase. In several countries the profits made from trading in looted antiquities have been used to finance terrorism.

Right One of more than 1,500 objects in the Oxus treasure, which dates from the Persian empire. A gold sheet showing a man, probably a priest, wearing tight trousers and tunic. This style of clothing was worn by Persians when hunting or in battle.

Below From the Oxus treasure. A gold roundel (sequin) that would have been sewn on to a garment. The clothing of Persian and Assyrian kings was often decorated in this way, as can be seen in the carved reliefs at Kalhu.

WAR DAMAGE IN THE NEAR EAST

The 1980–88 Iran–Iraq War and the 1990–1991 Gulf War caused terrible damage to the ancient monuments of Mesopotamia. The ziggurat built by Ur-Nammu at Ur and the Northwest Palace of Ashurnasirpal at Nineveh, for example, suffered direct hits.

The destruction at many important sites that do not have great monuments will not be known for a long time. Site exploration will also be drastically limited because of the danger of unexploded landmines and bombs.

LOOTING OF MUSEUMS

Since The Gulf War, museums at Basra, Kut, Amara, and Diwaniya in the south of Iraq, and at Erbil, Dohuk, and Suleimaniya in the northern regions, have been looted and burned. More than 4,000 objects are missing: Stone Age tools, cuneiform tablets, terracotta figurines, cylinder seals, and jewelry, covering all periods in Mesopotamian history. Descriptions of 2,000 stolen items have been recorded, but no object has so far been traced.

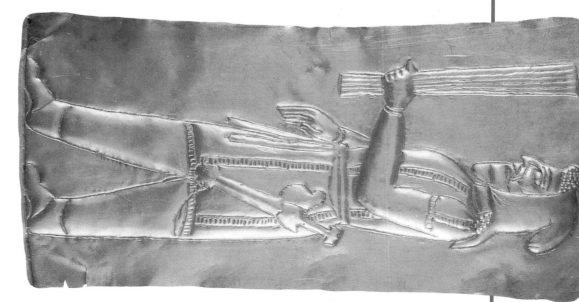

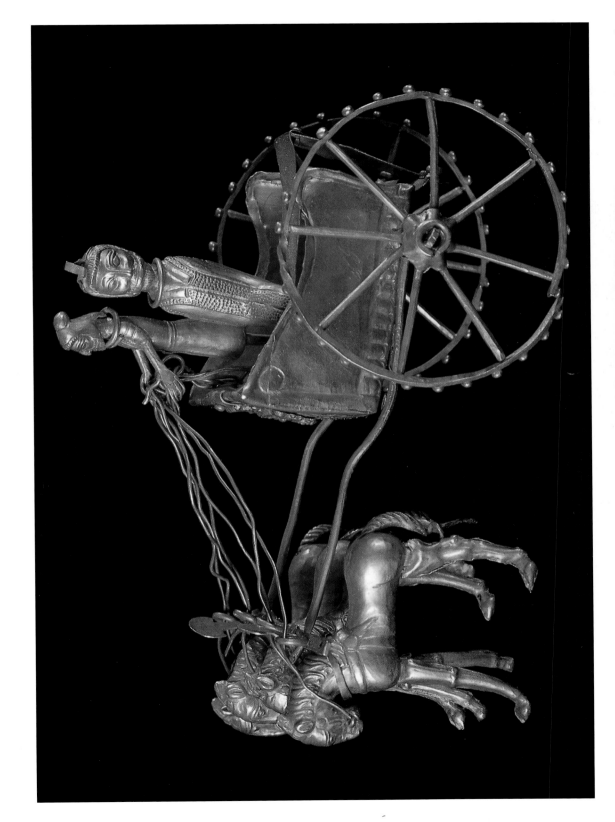

Above A gold model of a chariot, also from the Oxus treasure. The chariot is drawn by four horses and has on the front a head like that of the Egyptian god Bes. The model is less than 8in long.

Left This gold bracelet from the Oxus treasure is now in the Victoria and Albert Museum, London. The hollow spaces would have been filled with colored enamels. The bracelet must have been a popular design, for a similar one is shown in the stone carvings at Persepolis as part of the Bactrian tribute. The gold jewelry from the royal tombs at Kalhu is equally beautiful.

GLOSSARY

Aceramic A term given to the Neolithic period (c. 8500–7000 BCE) before pottery was invented.

Akkad The northern part of Mesopotamia. The southern area was called Sumer. Akkad was named after the city Agade, but by about 1800 BCE the region was called Babylonia.

Akkadian The dynasty founded by Sargon (c. 2300 BCE). Also the name of a Semitic language which was spoken in Mesopotamia as early as 3000 BCE.

Anatolia The highland plains of present-day central Turkey.

Assyria The northern part of modern Iraq, near the border with Turkey.

Assyrian A dialect of Akkadian spoken by the Assyrians. Also the name of a dynasty which has three main periods (c. 2000–612 BCE).

Babylonia The region of southern Mesopotamia which was called Akkad before about 1800 BCE.

Babylonian A dialect of Akkadian spoken by Babylonians. Also the name of the dynasty which ruled from about 2000 BCE to 750 BCE.

cuneiform The wedge-shaped script of Akkadian which was written on clay tablets and used throughout Mesopotamia and the Near East.

diorite A very hard black stone which was used to make statues.

dynasty A line of rulers usually from a single family or related through marriage.

Epi-Paleolithic The continuation of the Paleolithic or Old Stone Age culture after the last Ice Age. This period, which is sometimes called the Mesolithic, was followed by the Neolithic period.

Fertile Crescent The lands between the highland zones of Turkey and Iran and the deserts of Arabia, having 8in rainfall each year.

figurine A small statue made from wood, ivory, clay, or metal.

flint A hard stone used to make tools in the Paleolithic, Epi-Paleolithic and Neolithic periods.

king list A list of the names of kings and the lengths of their reigns. The best-known is the Sumerian King List, which records the dynasties ruling the cities of Sumer until 2000 BCE.

lapis lazuli A semiprecious blue stone that is only found in the mountains of Afghanistan.

law code A collection of laws recording the penalties for different crimes. The best-known law code is that of Hammurabi (c. 1800 BCE).

Levant The lands bordering the eastern Mediterranean, now modern Lebanon, Israel and coastal Syria.

Mesolithic The Middle Stone Age period between the Paleolithic or Old Stone Age and the Neolithic or New Stone Age. Also known as the Epi-Paleolithic.

Mesopotamia A Greek word meaning "between the rivers" and describing the lands in present-day Iraq, from south of modern Baghdad to the Gulf (Persian Gulf). The northern part of Mesopotamia was called Akkad, the southern lands Sumer.

microliths Very small chipped stone tools which first appear in the Mesolithic period.

Natufian A culture of the Epi-Paleolithic period in the Levant (c. 11,000–9300 BCE) when people began to grow grain.

Neolithic The New Stone Age (c. 9300–4000 BCE), which was divided into the Proto-Neolithic and Aceramic periods.

obsidian A natural volcanic glass from Anatolia that is much sharper than flint and was used to make tools.

Paleolithic The Old Stone Age, which ended with the last Ice Age in about 12,000 BCE. People obtained their food by hunting and gathering during this period.

pharaoh The title of the king of ancient Egypt.

Proto-Neolithic The period during the New Stone Age when grain was first grown (c. 9000–8500 BCE).

Semitic The language family that was widely spoken in Mesopotamia and the Near East and includes Akkadian and its dialects, Assyrian and Babylonian.

stele An upright stone or wooden slab, often decorated with carvings or bearing inscriptions.

Sumer The southern lands of Mesopotamia, reaching the Gulf (Persian Gulf), that were occupied by the Sumerians. The plain north of modern Baghdad, was called Akkad.

Sumerian The language which was spoken in Sumer by the Sumerians in about 4000 BCE. Sumerian does not belong to the Semitic language family.

tablet A small flat slab, usually made of clay, on which an inscription in cuneiform would be written.

tell An Arabic word for a mound made by the remains of ancient settlements. Often part of a place-name, as in Tell Madhhur.

ziggurat A high tower built in stepped stages with a temple at the top.

FURTHER READING

General works and picture books

John Curtis, *Ancient Persia* (British Museum Press), 2000.
William W. Hallo, *The Ancient Near East: A History* (Harcourt Brace), 1971.
Arnoldo Mondadori (ed.), *Virtual Archaeology* (Thames & Hudson), 1997.
Margaret Oliphant, *The Atlas of the Ancient World* (Marshall Editions), 1992.
Amiet Perce, *Art of the Ancient Near East* (Abrams), 1980.
Julian Reade, *Assyrian Sculpture* (British Museum Press), 1983.
Julian Reade, *Mesopotamia* (British Museum Press), 1991.
Georges Roux, *Ancient Iraq* (Viking Penguin), 1993.
Jonathan Tubb, *Bible Lands* (Dorling Kindersley), 1991.

Adult reference books

John Baines, *Atlas of Ancient Egypt* (Facts On File), 1980.
Norman Cantor (ed.), *The Pimlico Encyclopedia of the Middle Ages* (Pimlico), 1999.
Petr Charvet, *Mesopotamia Before History* (Routledge), 2002.
Dominique Collon, *Ancient Near Eastern Art* (British Museum Press), 1995.
O. R. Gurney, *The Hittites* (Viking Penguin), 1991.
David Nicolle, *History of Medieval Life* (Chancellor Press), 1997.
Joan C. Oates, *Babylon* (Thames & Hudson), 1986.
Michael Roaf, *Cultural Atlas of Mesopotamia and the Ancient Near East* (Facts On File), 1990.
John Rogerson, *The Atlas of the Bible* (Facts On File), 1984.

GAZETTEER

The gazetteer lists places and features, such as rivers or mountains, found on the maps. Each has a separate entry including a page and grid reference number. For example:

Abu Gosh 20 B2

Where a place also has an alternative name form this name is added to the entry before the page number. For example:

Alexandria (Ghazni) 89 E2

All features are shown in italic type. For example:

Anshan, d. 52 C2

A letter after the feature describes the kind of feature: *d.* district; *f.* feature; *i.* island; *mt.* mountain; *mts.* mountains; *r.* river

Abu Gosh 20 B2
Abu Hureyra 20 C3
Abu Salabikh 32 A3, 41 C2
Abu Salem 20 B2
Abydos 89 A3
Adab 41 C2, 47, 54 B2, 56 C2, 60 B2
Agade 52 B3, 56 C2
Aijalon 66 B2
Ain Ghazal 20 B2
Ain Mallaha 20 B2
Ain Gev I 20 B2
Akkad, d. 41 C2, 52 C3
Akshak 41 C2
al-Azizyeh 60 A3
al-Khiam 20 B2
Al-Untash-Napirisha (Choga Zanbil) 47
Alalakh 58 B2
Aleppo 58 B2, 65 B2, 72 B3
Alexandria 89 B2
Alexandria 89 C2
Alexandria 89 D1
Alexandria 89 E2
Alexandria 89 F1
Alexandria (Ghazni) 89 E2
Alexandria (Herat) 89 E2
Alexandria (Kandahar) 89 E2
Alexandria Eschata (Kokand) 89 F3
Alexandropolis 89 D2
Ali Kosh 20 E2, 29 E1
Alps, mts. 14 H6
Amanus Mts 41 A3
Amid 72 C3
Ammon, d. 66 C3, 72 B2
Amu Darya, r. 11 G3, 14 F3
An Nafud, f. 11 C1
Ana 65 C2, 72 C2
Anatolia, d. 10 B3, 14 B3, 20 A3, 25 B3
Ankara 89 B3

Anshan, d. 52 C2
Aornus 89 E2
Apamea 29 B2
Aphek 66 A3
Apku 47, 65 C2
Arabia, d. 11 D1, 14 C1, 84 B1
Arachosia, d. 85 F2, 89 E1
Arad of Beth-yeroham 66 B2
Aram, d. 66 C4, 72 B2
Araxes, r. 89 C3
Arbil 47, 58 D2, 65 C2, 72 D3, 89 C2
Aria, d. 85 F2, 89 E2
Armanum 52 A3
Armenia, d. 84 C3, 89 C2
Arpachiyeh 29 D2
Arrapha 65 C2, 72 D2
Arslantepe 29 C3
Asharne 72 B2
Ashdod 66 A2, 72 B1
Ashikli Huyuk 20 A4
Ashkelon 29 B1
Ashur 41 C3, 47, 52 B3, 56 B3, 58 D2, 65 C2, 72 D2
Asia Minor, d. 89 B2
Assyria, d. 72 C3, 84 C2
Awan 41 D2

Babylon 47, 52 B3, 54 A3, 56 C2, 58 D1, 60 A3, 65 C1, 72 D2, 82 C3, 84 C2, 89 C2
Babylonia, d. 72 D2, 84 C2, 89 C2
Bactria, d. 85 F2, 89 E2
Bad-tibira 41 C2, 54 C2
Badakhshan, d. 85 G2
Baghouz 29 C2
Baladruz 60 B4
Balikh, r. 52 B3
Basta 20 B2
Beer-sheba 66 A2
Beidha 20 B2
Beisamoun 20 B2
Belbasi 20 A3
Beth-Horon 66 B2
Beth-Shan 66 B3
Beth-Shemesh 66 A2
Bethel 66 B2
Bisutun 84 D2
Black Sea 11 C3, 14 B3, 15 F6, 25 B3, 82 B4, 84 B3, 89 B3
Borim 66 B3
Borsippa 47, 54 A3, 56 C2, 60 A3, 72 D2
Bouqras 20 C3
Byblos 29 B2, 41 A3, 58 B2, 72 B2

Cafer Huyuk 20 C4
Can Hasan 20 A3
Cappadocia, d. 84 B3
Carchemish 58 B2, 65 B2, 72 B3
Caria, d. 84 A2
Carmania, d. 84 E1, 89 D1

Carmel, Mt 20 B2, 66 B3
Caspian Sea 11 E3, 14 D3, 15 G6, 20 E4, 25 D3, 29 E3, 41 E3, 52 C4, 72 E3, 82 D4, 84 D3, 89 D2
Caucasus Mts 11 D3, 82 C4
Cedar Mt 52 A3
Chagar Bazar 29 C2
Chatal Huyuk 29 A2
Chayonu 20 C4
Choga Bonut 20 E2
Choga Mami 29 D1
Choga Zanbil *see* Al-Untash-Napirisha
Chorasmia, d. 85 E2
Cilicia, d. 82 B3, 89 B2
Crete, i. 84 A2, 89 A2
Cyprus, i. 10 B2, 20 A3, 25 A2, 29 A2, 52 A3, 72 A2, 84 B2, 89 B2
Cyrene 89 A2

Damascus 66 C4, 72 B2, 89 B2
Dasht-e Kavir, f. 11 E2
Dasht-e Lut, f. 11 F2
Dead Sea 15 F6, 29 B1, 41 A2, 52 A1, 58 B1, 66 B2, 72 B1, 84 B2
Deh-i No 47
Der 41 C2, 60 B3, 72 D2
Derbent 89 E2
Dilbat 54 A3, 56 C2
Dilmun, d. 52 C2
Diyala, r. 41 C3, 58 D2, 65 C2
Dor 66 A3
Dothan 66 B3
Drangiana, d. 84 E1
Dur-Katlimmu 65 B2
Dur-Kurigalzu 47, 60 A3, 65 C1, 72 D2
Dur-Sharrukin (Khorsabad) 47, 72 D3

Ebla 41 A3, 52 A3, 58 B2
Edom, d. 66 B1, 72 B1
Egypt, d. 10 B1, 14 B1, 52 A2, 72 A1, 82 B2, 84 A1, 89 A1
Elam, d. 11 E2, 41 D2, 52 C2, 72 E2, 84 D2
Elburz Mts 11 E2
Emesa 89 B2
Emuthal, d. 56 C2
Eridu 29 E1, 41 D2, 47, 54 C1, 56 C1
Eshnunna 41 C2, 56 C2
Euphrates, r. 11 C2, 14 C2, 20 C2, 29 C2, 32 B1, 41 B3, 47, 52 B3, 54 A2, 56 B2, 58 C2, 60 A2, 65 B2, 72 C2, 82 C3, 84 C2, 89 C2

Galilee, Sea of 66 B3
Gandara, d. 85 F2
Ganj Dareh 20 E3
Gaugamela 89 C2
Gaza 66 A2, 72 B1, 89 B2

Gedrosia, d. 89 E1
Gezer 66 A2
Ghazni *see* Alexandria
Gibeon 66 B2
Gilgal 66 B3
Girsu 41 D2, 54 C2, 56 C2, 60 B2
Gobi, f. 14 J6
Godin Tepe 41 D3
Granicus 89 A3
Great Zab, r. 11 D2, 20 D3, 41 C3, 58 D2
Great Arad 66 B2
Greece, d. 89 A2
Gritille 20 C3
Gulf, The 11 E1, 14 D1, 15 B2, 20 E1, 25 D1, 41 D1, 47, 52 C2, 56 D1, 60 C1, 72 E1, 82 D2, 84 D1, 89 D1
Gutium, d. 41 C3

Habur, r. 11 C2, 20 C3, 29 C2, 41 B3, 52 B3, 58 C2
Hacilar 20 A3
Hajji Muhammad 29 D1
Hama 29 B2, 72 B2
Hamadan 82 D3, 84 D2, 89 C2
Hamazi 41 C3
Hamman 47
Hana, d. 56 B3
Haradum 56 B3
Harhar 72 E2
Harlicarnassus 89 A2
Harran 58 C2, 65 B2, 72 C3, 82 C3
Hasanlu 29 D2, 41 C3
Hatula 20 B2
Hazor 66 B4
Hecatompylos 89 D2
Hejaz, f. 11 C1
Herat *see* Alexandria
Himalayas, mts. 14 J5
Hindanu 72 C2
Hit 65 C1
Huleh, Lake 66 B4

Imleihiyeh 60 B4
Indus, d. 85 F1
Indus, r. 14 F1, 82 F2, 85 F1, 89 E1
Iona, d. 84 A2
Isin 54 B2, 56 C2, 60 B2
Israel, d. 66 B3, 72 B2
Issus 89 B2

Jarmo 20 D3, 29 D2
Jericho 20 B2, 66 B2
Jerusalem 66 B2, 72 B1, 82 B3, 84 B2, 89 B2
Jezreel 66 B3
Joppa 66 A3
Jordan, r. 66 B3
Judah, d. 66 B2, 72 B1

Kalhu 47, 65 C2, 72 D3
Kandahar *see* Alexandria
Kar-Tukulti-Ninurta 47, 65 C2
Kara Kum, f. 11 F3
Karim Shahir 20 D3
Kebara 20 B2
Khafajeh 52 B3
Khan Bani Sa'ad 60 A3
Khorsabad *see* Dur-Sharrukin
Kilizu 65 C2
Kiriath-jearim 66 B2
Kish 41 C2, 47, 52 B3, 54 A3, 56 C2, 60 A3
Kisurra 54 B2
Kizil Irmak, r. 11 B3,14 B3, 52 A4, 58 B3
Kokand *see* Alexandria Eschata
Kokola 89 E1
Kul Tepe 29 D2
Kulishkhinash 65 B2
Kutha 54 A3, 56 C2, 60 A3, 72 D2

Lachish 66 A2
Lagash 41 D2, 52 C2, 56 C2
Larnaca 72 A2
Larsa 47, 54 B2, 56 C1, 60 B2
Lebanon Mts 84 B2
Levant, d. 11 B2/C2, 14 B2
Libyan Desert 82 A2
Little Zab, r. 20 D3
Lower Sea 52 C2
Lydia, d. 82 A4, 84 A1

Macedon, d. 89 A3
Magan, d. 52 D1
Maka, d. 84 E1
Malatya 65 B3
Mananaim 66 B3
Maracanda (Samarkand) 89 E2
Marad 54 A3
Marashi, d. 52 C2
Mari 41 B3, 47, 52 B3, 56 B3
Mashkan-shapir 54 B3, 56 C2
Me-Turnat 60 B4
Media, d. 72 E2, 82 E3, 84 D2, 89 D2
Mediterranean Sea 10 B2, 14 A2, 15 F6, 20 A2, 25 A2, 29 A2, 52 A3, 58 A1, 72 A2, 82 A3, 84 A2, 89 A2
Megiddo 58 B1, 66 B3
Memphis 82 B2, 84 B1, 89 B1
Mersin 29 B2
Mesopotamia, d. 11 D2, 14 C2, 20 D3, 89 C2
Millet Mergi 72 D3
Moab, d. 66 B2, 72 B1
Muqdadiyeh 60 B4
Mureybet 20 C3

Nahal Hemar 20 B2
Najafehabad 72 E2
Nemrik 20 D3
Neo-Babylonia, d. 82 C3
Neribtum 56 C2

Nila, r. 10 BI, 14 BI, 20 AI, 82
  B2, 84 BI, 89 BI
Nineveh 29 D2, 41 C3, 47, 52
  B3, 58 D2, 65 C2, 72 B3,
  89 C2
Nippur 32 A3, 41 C2, 47, 52
  B3, 54 B3, 56 C2, 58 DI,
  60 B2, 72 D2
Nisibin 72 C3
Niya, d. 58 B2
Nubia, d. 84 BI
Nuzi 41 C3, 65 C2, 58 D2

Oman, Gulf of 11 FI
Opis 60 A3
Oracle of Amman 89 AI
Orontes, r. 58 B2

Palegawra 20 D3
Palmyra 72 C2
Parthia, d. 84 D2, 89 D2
Pasargadae 82 D3, 84 D2, 89
  D2
Pella 20 B2
Penuel 66 B3
Persepolis 84 DI, 89 DI
Persia, d. 14 D2, 82 D2, 84 DI,
  89 DI
Philia 29 A2
Philista 66 A2
Phrygia, d. 72 A3
Peros, Kingdom of, d. 89 F2

Qadesh 58 B2
Qarqar 72 B2
Qatar 15 BI
Qatara *see* Tell al-Rimah
Qermez Dere 20 D3
Que, d. 72 B3

Ramoth-Gilead 66 C3
Ras Shamra *see* Ugarit

Rayy *see* Rhagae
Red Sea 11 CI, 14 BI, 15 F5, 25
  BI, 52 AI, 82 CI, 84 BI, 89
  BI
Rhagae (Rayy) 89 D2
Rosh Zin 20 B2
Rosh Horesha 20 B2

Sagartia *see* Carmania
Sahara, f. 14 H5
Sais 82 B3
Salam Pak 60 A3
Samaria 66 B3, 72 B2
Samarkand *see* Maracanda
Samarra 29 D2
Sar-i Pol-i Zohab 60 B4
Sardis 82 A4, 84 A3, 89 A2
Sattagydia, d. 85 F2
Scythia, d. 84 C3, 85 E3
Shadikanni 65 B2
Shaduppum 56 C2
Shanidar 20 D3
Sharuhen 66 A2
Shatt al-Gharraf, r. 32 B3
Shatt al-Hilla, r. 32 A2
Shechem 66 B3
Sheriltum, d. 52 D2
Shibaniba 65 C2
Shubat-Enlil 47
Shunem 66 B3
Shuruppak 41 C2
Shusharra 29 D2
Sidon 66 B4, 72 B2
Silver Mt 52 A3
Simurrum 52 B3
Sinai d. 10 BI, 25 AI
Sinjar 72 C3
Sippar 41 C2, 47, 52 B3, 54 A4,
  56 C2, 58 DI, 60 A3, 65 CI,
  72 D2
Socoh 66 B3
Sogdia, d. 85 F3

Sogdiana, d. 89 E2
Soli 89 B2
South China Sea 14 J4
Sparta 89 A2
Subartu, d. 52 B3
Sudan 15 F5
Suhu, d. 56 B3
Sumer, d. 41 D2, 52 C2
Susa 41 D2, 47, 52 C3, 60 C2,
  72 E2, 82 D3, 84 D2, 89
  C2
Syria, d. 11 C2, 14 B2, 66 B4
Syrian Desert 11 C2, 14 C2, 41
  B3, 72 C2

Taanach 66 B3
Tama 82 C2
Tarsus 29 B2, 41 A3, 58 B2, 72
  B3, 82 B3, 89 B2
Taurus Mts 10 B2
Taxila 89 F2
Tekoa 66 B2
Tell Agrab 41 C2
Tell al-Fakhariyeh *see*
  Washukanni
Tell al-Hawa 47
Tell al-Hayyad 32 B3
Tell al-Kirbasi 60 CI
Tell al-Rimah (Qatara) 47, 58
Tell al-Sawwan 29 D2
Tell al Ubaid 41 D2
Tell Aswad 20 B2
Tell Aswad 20 C3
Tell Awayli 29 DI, 32 BI
Tell Brak 29 C2, 41 B3, 52 B3,
  58 C2
Tell Dlehim 32 A2
Tell Halaf 29 C2
Tell Hasan 29 D2
Tell Jokha 41 C2
Tell Judeideh 29 B2

Tell Mismar 32 BI
Tell Mohammed Arab 65 C2
Tell Muhammad 56 C2, 60 A3
Tell Ramad 20 B2, 29 BI
Tell Shmid 32 B2
Tell Umm Dabaghiyeh 29 D2
Telul al-Thalathat 29 D2
Tepe Gawra 29 D2
Tepe Giyan 29 E2, 41 D3
Tepe Guran 20 E2, 29 EI
Tepe Sarab 29 E2
Terqa 72 C2
Thapsacus 89 B3
Thebes 82 B2, 84 BI, 89 A2
Thrace, d. 89 A3
Tigris, r. 11 D2, 14 C2, 20 D2,
  29 D2, 32 B3, 41 C3, 47,
  52 B3, 54 B3, 56 C3, 58
  D2, 60 B2, 65 CI, 72 E2,
  82 C3, 84 C2, 89 C2
Til Barsip 41 B3
Tirzah 66 B3
Tushpa 72 D3
Tuttul 52 B3
Tutub 41 C2, 56 C2
Tyre 66 B4, 72 B2, 89 B2

Ugarit (Ras Shamra) 20 B3, 29
  B2, 58 B2, 65 A2
Umm al-Aqarib 32 B2
Umma 32 B2, 41 C2, 52 B2,
  56 C2
Upper Sea 52 A3
Ur 15 G6, 29 EI, 41 D2, 47,
  52 C2, 54 CI, 56 CI, 60
  B2, 72 EI, 82 D3
Urartu, d. 72 D3
Urmia, Lake 14 D2, 15 G6, 20
  D3, 29 D2, 41 C3, 47, 52
  C3, 58 D2, 65 C2, 72 D3,
  82 D3, 84 C2

Uruk 32 BI, 41 C2, 47, 52 B2,
  54 B2, 56 C2, 58 DI, 60 B2
Van, Lake 14 C3, 15 F6, 20 D4,
  29 D3, 47, 52 B4, 58 D3,
  65 C3, 72 D3, 82 C4, 84
  C3
Wadi Hasa 20 B2
Wadi Dubai B 20 B2
Warium, d. 56 C3
Washukanni (Tell al-Fakhariyeh)
  58 C2, 65 B2
Yaharisha 65 B2
Yarim Tepe I and II 29 D2
Yarmuti 52 A3
Yelkhi 60 B4
Zabalam 54 B2, 56 C2
Zagros Mountains 11 D2, 25 C2,
  29 EI, 41 D2, 65 DI
Zahara 52 C3
Zarephath 66 B4
Zarzi 20 D3
Zawi Chemi Shanidar 20 D3
Zemaraim 66 B2
Zubeidi 60 B4

INDEX